Man

of the

House

...a Gold Star Family's Journey

M. Patrick

Names of persons and places are changed to protect privacy

Dedication

Many stories have been written, rightly so, about the lives of our "Heroes" — those military members killed in service to our country.

This memoir-based novel serves as one example of the lives many "Gold Star" families are left to navigate without their hero.

Told through the thoughts of a young widow and events recalled by a son, this story includes moments of anxiety, self-doubt, struggle, failure, success, and survival, with occasions of humor.

The son's stories of his meanderings and anecdotes about adventures and misadventures provide some insights into a life unguided by a father's wisdom.

This family's story parallels innumerable family stories in time immemorial.

I hope our story, though uniquely ours, provides some encouragement to other families who must suddenly begin their "Gold Star" journey.

Our Gold Star Journey

It's My Party

Wow! I can't imagine how DW located so many people who have been such an important part of my life. And how could she have found all the many friends and acquaintances whom I have known since my pre-DW years, but they all seem to be here along with our many mutual friends. As usual, she is hugging each guest, and they all seem to be crying! Tears of love, no doubt.

The decorations are fantastic, and the musicians are my favorites. As she has done on so many other special occasions, DW has dressed me in my very best finery so as not to embarrass either of us. What a perfect party for me!

Since most of the guests are actually dead and gone, I'm guessing this is really a masquerade party celebrating my eventual passing. But, the masks are so real! Where did she find such perfect actors to play those who have passed on before me? They walk the same and talk the same — exactly as I remember.

Those few guests who are still alive wear no mask, though they might look better if they did. Unlike the actors who are wearing masks depicting friends at younger ages, the faces of guests without masks evidence the reality of lives lived long.

I see my beloved twins, Gus, Kay S, Kay and Gregory R, Ronnie T, Jimmy L, Darrell M and Don S—all palavering in their respective groups! There's Bernie, Sally, and Jackie (comparing notes, no doubt). Carol, Mom, favorite daughter and family, and Kelly and Janise are here! Denis W, Jon S, and Dave R are huddling suspiciously! I hope Gene B and Ron S arrive soon. This is going to be the best night ever!

"One-dollar-Sarge" is showing his empty wallet to some priests, who seem somewhat doubtful of his veracity.

My father must be here somewhere. I'll keep looking! I may finally get to meet him! Our "Gold Star" family may be reunited at last!

Wow, again! George Shearing is starting to perform. I first heard his music my freshman year in college in Dave's dorm room, where George's music emanated from Dave's old (circa 1958) portable record player. It was the most beautiful music I had ever heard.

Guests are gathering around George and his quintet for "All This and Heaven Too." DW just announced that we will also hear Dave Brubeck and others of my favorite musicians throughout this evening.

I hope jazz pianist, Emmet Cohen, plays "Somewhere Over the Rainbow." And maybe Louis Armstrong will perform "When the Saints go Marching In." George's "Lullaby of Birdland" would also be good to hear.

If the party lasts long enough, I will visit with each guest, some of whom I wish to share my entire life experience. With others, I may need to obscure, or even deny, certain events. And I want to hear their life stories. There are so many things I need to learn to help me make sense of my life and understand its many, nagging mysteries.

Or, I may simply reminisce alone and accept the mysteries as they are. Maybe I'll find an unused mask and circulate among the guests to overhear their stories.

Perhaps I'll enjoy a sip of Dave's Irish whiskey.

If I can just climb out of this box...

(My Dream)

****

Our Story

Aug 18,1941 At 11:00 AM in a very busy Mercy Hospital, I came into this world kicking and screaming, leaving my Mom with a forever abdominal scar, though Mom probably wasn't thinking about this at the time .

More likely, she was angry at my dad for being absent from my introduction to the world. Of course, he had the usual reason father's give for missing important lifetime events — he was working, in another state, earning the money to pay for my introduction. For that, he deserves some credit.

And so my life began...

Backstory Mom and dad met in high school in a basic, small, farm community in central Iowa. The community was so small it lacked a town square, but it compensated totally with a central town triangle. Class sizes were so small that most students participated in all activities in order to field teams in sports and other activities. Mom played six-girl basketball. Dad played in the band and on the baseball team, as did his brothers, Bill and Ray. They also participated in band and school plays. There were plenty of opportunities, beyond the classroom, for students to get together and socialize. Mom and dad were known to be excellent at socializing.

Mom was born December 4, 1915, and grew up on a crop and livestock farm - 160 acres of bountiful farmland that sufficed adequately for two brothers, Grandfather Weaver and Great Uncle Ben, to raise their respective families in reasonable, though not luxurious, comfort. Comfort, that is, if one defines it as a good meal after a long, hard day's work. Life on the farm was not easy, but it enabled family members to eat well, own good automobiles, and become relatively well-educated.

Regarding education, after high school, Mom followed her older sister into nurses training, for an understandable reason — to avoid staying on the farm and spending a lifetime cooking, washing, and cleaning for those hard-working men.

She would not have had to cook for her brother, Dillon, however, as he eventually found his way off the farm and made a career in the banking industry

Dad was born February 8, 1915. His father was a coal miner/manager, and the family moved several times, whenever required by his employer. At some point, the family located in Mom's community where the brothers and their sister, Lena, also went to Mom's school. There were many coal mines in this and the surrounding states in the 1930's, so jobs were plentiful. The brothers soon decided, after working in the local mine during high school, they were not destined to be miners, and life took them each in different directions.

As love does, love blossomed between Mom and dad during high school. Graduation finally arrived and both went forth into the near-adult world of higher education. Mom went to nurses training and dad went to pharmacy school at university 200 miles distant. Letters found years later in Mom's desk, after her passing, indicate neither passion nor poetry were in short supply between them. There were pet names. There were weekend trips hitchhiked by dad to see Mom - for understandable reasons.

In time, college graduations (August 15, 1938 from nurses training for Mom and June 5, 1939 from Pharmacy School for dad) were celebrated, a marriage was consummated, and their real adult life began. At the same time, the winds of a world war were stirring.

Both began their careers, but still separated by 100 miles.

Sister Carol arrived on May 10, 1940. When I was born, we became a complete family of four, living in our new "Hometown" house.

Dad then joined a friend in ownership of a small neighborhood pharmacy, and Mom resumed her nursing career in Hometown. Dad soon left the pharmacy and became a pharmaceutical sales rep for the Upjohn Company, being on the road days at a time.

But, as the world war progressed, dad decided it was his patriotic duty to serve in the military, and he enlisted in the Naval Reserve in December 1943.

Upon being commissioned an Ensign, and having completed the needed training, he was assigned to LCT (6) 729 as "officer-in-charge" and soon found himself in combat in the Pacific theatre, delivering needed war materials to troops during island landings.

On February 16, 1945, while delivering such war materials onto Corregidor Island, Philippines, dad received lethal enemy machine gun fire — and died.

Our Gold Star Journey had begun…

Feb 1945   Telegram

WESTERN UNION

"The Secretary of War desires to express his deepest regret that your husband, Ensign Harry Elmo Patrick, was killed in action on 16 February 1945 in the Philippines…

Feb 1945   Man of the House   It was an unusually warm day for February, and I had been playing outside in the mulberry tree between our house and the neighbor's. The neighbor suddenly ushered Carol and me into her house, without explanation. While we didn't understand why, we knew something important was happening when grandparents, aunts and uncles, and Mom's friends began arriving. Soon thereafter, we were allowed to go home.

I wasn't yet four years old, so I did not understand the meaning of the hugs, the whispered "hellos," the mournful tears, and Mom crying in her bedroom. As a five year-old, Carol was more aware, but she did not share with me what had happened. She was busy acting as the "lady of the house," taking care of our guests.

According to my Uncle Dillon, I was now the "man of the house."

Daylight passed and most guests departed, except for Aunt Susie, who stayed to comfort Mom and look after us.

Mom stayed in her bedroom. She just wanted to be alone.

Spring 1945   A Flag and Three Boxes   The following weeks were not joyful, but the days seemed more settled.

Mom was crying less and often explained to us that our father was never coming home again, and we would now be an incomplete family of three.

Then one day, a boxed United States flag arrived from the President via USPS mail. Mom would not let us open it.

Days later, a knock on the door caused Mom more distress. Three boxes had arrived.

Two men in coveralls unloaded the boxes from an unmarked gray truck. They worked quickly and did not speak. They knew what the boxes contained, as they had delivered many identical boxes before, and there was always the same response from the people who received the shipment — no smiles, no laughter — offering only a token, courteous "thank-you" for the men's help.

The boxes were heavy and sturdy, having been built by men who knew the boxes would have to travel long distances. Built of dark white lumber, they had gray numbers and letters stenciled on their outsides. The builders of the boxes knew the contents needed to be protected from the scourges of time, travel, and repeated handling by many men and machines that might neither know nor worry about their contents. These builders must have been very caring men to have done such a good job, having built so many of these boxes in the months and years prior to building our three.

After carrying the boxes to our basement, the men in coveralls quickly departed.

Mom had not let us open the boxed flag, and now she wouldn't let us open the boxes. She sat on the basement steps daily for hours, staring at the boxes and crying.

With the help and understanding of our relatives, Mom decided she desperately needed some time alone, so Carol and I stayed with our Great Uncle Ben and Great Aunt Alma on their farm for a few days. Our love for the farm softened the trauma of leaving Mom temporarily. Carol told me Mom would feel much better when we returned home.

Such was not to be the case

1945 Taylor Time Mom soon decided living in town and attending a neighborhood Catholic school would be better for us than more time spent on the farm. With assistance of Catholic Charities, Carol and I then found ourselves staying with a family, the Taylors, who had been recommended by a Catholic Charities official and who lived close to the school. Taylor time turned out to be quite short, however, as our treatment there was not exemplary.

I vaguely remember the time we were living with the Taylor family. I was younger than 5 years old. Although Carol would probably remember the events which resulted in our being there and for how long, I have only this one clear memory — a memory which leaves me to wonder how many other children may have experienced the same sadistic, unique, special form of "Taylor discipline" I received. It also makes me wonder what the Taylor's childhoods must have been like that they would perpetrate such discipline on a child.

The Taylors required us to be outside the house during the day, entering only for meals. Following those instructions, I was playing outside on a beautiful spring afternoon — blue skies and sunshine. Nearby street construction held my attention, especially as a giant road grader performed its duties on the project. Tractors, trucks, road graders, and other large motorized equipment always fascinated me.

This fascination was, perhaps, partly responsible for what happened, although my fear of asking the Taylors for access to the house was also contributory. As I watched while leaning against a wooden telephone pole, the road grader moved — and so did my bowel! What a mess! Embarrassment was not my greatest concern, however— anticipation of the Taylor's punishment was! So, I kept my distress to myself.

When finally allowed into the house at the end of the day, my keepers discovered my situation. Angrily, and with strange delight, they jointly exacted their unique form of discipline and rubbed the messy content of my underwear onto my nose, requiring me to leave it there until bedtime (one of the few times in my life when I wished I could seriously hurt someone)!

1945/1946/1947 The Farm Fortunately, our Great Uncle Ben and Great Aunt Alma visited us at the Taylor's a few days after the traumatic incident. Upon hearing how the Taylors were treating us, they took us to stay at their farm until a better arrangement could be determined.

The stay turned into several months and allowed us to experience both the beauty of the rural life and the thrill of a country school and school bus.

Over the years The South Farmstead My early experiences on the family farm engendered a desire to be there whenever possible, which was usually summers and Christmas vacations (until I reached the teen/city years). What a wonderful place to experience life! Clean air, close to nature, hard work, animal life, great fun, good food, common folk.

Those 160 acres of rich, central-Iowa farm land provided a livelihood for several generations. My grandfather and great uncle were raised there, as were my mother, her brother, Dillon, and their half-sister, Susie. By the time I was born, my grandfather, "Pop"Weaver, and his third wife, Neva, lived on the original, south farmstead, and Great Uncle Ben, and Great Aunt Alma, lived on the newer, north farmstead. Great Uncle Grover had left the farm to become a barber and live in a small nearby town, and he had committed suicide before I was born.

Vacations. Holidays. Whenever an opportunity arose, I was at the farm. While I usually stayed at the south farmstead with the grandparents, both the grandparents and the "greats" were outstanding teachers, providers, protectors, and disciplinarians.

The kitchen was central to daily life. Pop made a great chili! Grandma made a fantastic angel food cake with a pineapple powder frosting! Homemade ice cream was devoured there!

Not so enjoyable were the once-weekly baths, which always occurred on Saturday night — in a galvanized tub, in the middle of the kitchen! Water was heated on the wood burning stove (also used for all cooking) and poured into the tub. Pop would bathe first, then Carol, and then me. Ugh! The water had become quite icky by the time it was my turn! Grandma Neva would provide any necessary scrubbing.

Curiously, I don't recall Grandma ever taking a turn in the tub.

Fortunately for me, these were years of transition for rural homes, as indoor plumbing soon revolutionized farmers' bathing protocols, while also eliminating both the outside "two-seater" and the nighttime, inside "porcelain potty."

There were stifling "kid rules" to be followed, e.g., "Don't listen to neighbors' conversations on the party line," and "Kids are to be seen but not heard." Horrible rules! No way could we develop good verbal communications skills following those rules!

The farm is where I learned to drive. Pop taught me first on the Ford tractor. Uncle Ben taught me later in the Ford F-1 pickup. This was long before farm vehicles had air conditioning, power steering, a radio, GPS, etc.

Grandma Neva taught me to retrieve eggs from the chickens' undersides (driving tractors and trucks was much more fun!). The eggs were then stored in a small, enclosed out-building, to be picked up weekly by a gentleman who sold them in the city as "farm fresh eggs." (How fresh could eggs be after being stored in a small, enclosed out-building for a week of hot summer days? Today's Truth-in-Advertising laws would require him to advertise "eggs with a touch of red"!)

Grandmother Neva facilitated another learning experience for me — smoking Chesterfield cigarettes. She seemed to enjoy smoking and would fill the kitchen with a thick haze while conducting her daily domestic duties. Those Chesterfields were long and strong, and when she wasn't looking, I would "borrow" one from her package and sneak down behind the barn to enjoy, between my coughing and hacking, that wonderful, adult experience of smoke destroying my lungs. Such a thrill!

The barn was my entertainment center. It was filled with outdated equipment, tools, and horse tack utilized years before tractors replaced the beasts of burden. A really great day on the farm included "saddling up" — i.e., mounting an old leather saddle stored on a stall wall, grabbing the bridles tied to the adjoining post, and "Hi Ho Silver-ing away" the day. I was "...that masked man" on those days!

The upstairs hay mow was the rural precursor to the McDonalds restaurant Play Place. The carefully stacked bales of hay and the ropes and pulleys that got them there provided a fairly safe venue for climbing, jumping, and sliding. As "Superman," I flew through the mow's air, clinging firmly to the ropes. When secrecy was needed for other youthful activities, the mow was the perfect place.

Saturday nights were special for Pop. After the weekly bath, Pop would drive to the town tavern and, over an appropriate number of beers, vigorously debate with other farmers about weather, crops, market prices for cattle, pigs, corn, and soy beans, equipment types and prices, politics, and other timely issues. And, finally, with all issues settled, Pop would load his upcoming week's case of beer into the car and head for home.

Every Saturday night, while I slept, Grandma Neva sat up, waited, and worried about Pop until he arrived home.

On any other night, when visitors stopped at the farm, Pop and the visiting men would gather at the barn, enjoy a beer, and solve the world's current problems, which mostly involved taking turns cussing the democrats, then the republicans, and then arguing about whether Ford or General Motors built the better cars. These discussions were loudly punctuated with their highly succinct "farmer's" vocabulary.

Nights on the south farmstead could be scary. The yard light, perched high atop a wooden pole, cast eerie shadows through the trees and against the buildings. Animal vocals and other strange noises pierced the dark. When jumping into bed after having just spent the evening with Grandma listening to "The FBI in Peace and War" and other radio broadcasts about all the evil in the country and all the assorted criminals running loose, it was best to just pull the covers over my head, close my eyes, and pray for quick and safe sleep.

And morning always came...

Over the years The North Farmstead Nights on the north farmstead were different. There seemed to be fewer shadows, and Aunt Alma didn't listen to those radio shows about evil happenings. Lying in bed each night, I would hear the blast of the whistle on the train passing near the far side of the farm and fall asleep wondering why that train passed at the same time each night, where it was going, and who was on it. In the mornings, I would hear the birds chirping in the meadow. The north farmstead always felt safer and more comfortable.

It is from whence Carol and I rode the old, worn yellow school bus to and from grade school.

Though it seemed like a very long walk down the lane from the farm house to the mailbox, where the bus would pick us, it was actually shorter than the walk from our childhood home to the school in our hometown. But, in the cold of winter, through the knee-high snow, this distance seemed much more challenging. It was worthwhile, however, as there was always a reward awaiting me on the bus — my "first love" twin sisters. So what if they were eight-graders, and I was only a first-grader. I'm sure they felt the same way about me!

Sunday evenings after dinner, Aunt Alma prepared the best treat — a vanilla, ice cream milkshake which we joyfully consumed as we strained our eyes watching The Ed Sullivan Show on the 12-inch, black-and-white screen!

Uncle Ben was a skilled craftsman, like most farmers of that era. If something needed to be made of steel, Ben was the master. He warned me to never pick up anything he placed on the sidewalk outside the forge room. I learned quickly why he gave me the warning when I picked up a newly forged tractor trailer pin and suffered third degree burns on my fingertips.

In an upstairs bathroom, Uncle Ben provided haircuts for all family members. Hanging on the side of his barber's chair was the "strop" on which his straight razors were sharpened. On one especially difficult occasion, Uncle Ben explained to me how that strop was also useful for applying any needed discipline.

Uncle Ben's right index finger was apparently attached by a nerve to his right leg, because when one of us youngsters would, accordingly, respond to his "Pull my Finger!" instruction, his right leg would simultaneously elevate, followed by an explosion of sound and odor. Always shocking to us youngsters, while always disgustingly entertaining to the adults present, this seemed to provide Uncle Ben one of his greatest thrills!

Depression-era farmers treated their farm equipment very tenderly. All equipment had to last forever. When teaching me to drive the Ford F-1 pickup, Uncle Ben dictated it was appropriate to "coast" to all stops, using brakes only as a last resort. With him along riding shotgun, my coasting had to begin so far away from a stop that it seemed we would never get there. On the positive side, his equipment aged quite slowly.

Just as he conserved his equipment, Uncle Ben also conserved his cigars. Never lighting it, Uncle Ben's cigar would last all day as it hung in his mouth. It only grew shorter when he would cut off and dispose of the saliva-soaked end before putting the remainder back into his mouth.

Uncle Ben had skills far beyond farming. He was also a musician and a cowboy. He played drums in a band, and he could twirl a lariat around both him and Billy, his horse, while sitting atop Billy. He had served his country for a time in the Army. A dapper man of the times, he met and eventually married Aunt Alma. The resulting "alienation of affections" lawsuit ended with a financial settlement to her previous husband.

Billy had lived on the farm many years before I arrived. He was Uncle Ben's favorite animal. When I was ten, Uncle Ben finally allowed me to ride Billy, with the admonition: "Do not run him!" I promised accordingly, and my promise lasted until I got around the corner of the grove beyond where Uncle Ben could see me. Poor Billy!

Poor me! Uncle Ben was not to be fooled. But, it was worth it! I was a real cowboy while I was on Billy for that once-in-a-lifetime, albeit very short, ride.

The wives of farmers had challenging lives — birthing at home, cooking on wood-fueled stoves, farm choring (ever see the skin damage to a farm wife's arms resulting from the pecking assaults of chickens while gathering eggs?), no air conditioning, endless amounts of dust from fields and dirt roads, scrubbing laundry on wash boards, boiling all consumable water on the stove, etc. Aunt Alma's labors with laundry were exhausting just to watch.

Farm fashions were vastly different from city fashions — e.g., Uncle Ben's and Pop's combination top and bottom, pale white (probably very white when originally purchased) underwear, with access openings both front and back facilitating needed bodily functions; one-piece bib overalls; hand sewn-shirts and dresses made from feed bags; winter hats with ear flaps; five-buckle galoshes; high-top brown shoes with laces.

Like Pop, Uncle Ben enjoyed Saturday nights in town. And like Grandma Neva, Aunt Alma enjoyed those Saturday nights alone at home. Alma and Neva went to town for church services on Sunday morning, while Pop and Uncle Ben stayed home. The schedule seemed to work well for everyone!

The farm was a wonderful place to visit. Everyone was very friendly in the country, as evidenced daily by the hand waves between farmers and drivers as cars sped past fields on the gravel roads. I visited as often as possible.

Curiously, for all the time Carol and I spent there, no one ever mentioned our father!

1946/1947 Boarding School Mom made a difficult decision soon after Carol and I returned home from our grade school time on the farm. She had already arranged to return to work, would be starting soon, and didn't want to leave Carol and me at the farm nor with a daytime babysitter. She felt it would take all of her energy to refresh her nursing skills, and she needed more time to prepare for returning to a normal, controlled life. So, she decided to place us in a good boarding school until she was ready to take proper care of us.

Carol and I were soon packing our bags again and climbing into a stranger's car for the long ride to our new, "temporary" home — a children's home, operated by an order of Catholic nuns. Unbeknownst to us, Mom had suffered a relapse and was simultaneously self-admitted to a nearby facility.

Though they seemed very nice at the beginning, I soon developed a serious dislike for the nuns. They were always giving me instructions, and their rules were very strict. I never liked being given instructions before I met the nuns, and I was liking it even less as the days went by at the school.

However, I did like "candy Fridays" — the only day the school's candy store was open. Carol and I usually received enough money, sent from our mother, to purchase an adequate supply for the coming week. We also liked our new friends and sometimes shared our candy with those who had none.

A highlight for the boys was singing a special song as we marched around the gym—

> Tramp, tramp, tramp, the boys are marching,
> Here comes Hitler to the door.
> If we ever get a chance
> We will kick him in the pants.
> And there won't be Hitler anymore.

I didn't like Hitler, either.

What seemed like an eternity at the boarding school ended when, one wonderful day, a kindly nun told us to pack our bags — we were going home!

1947 ff 205 H Avenue (over the years) We three returned to our Hometown home - 205 H Avenue.

At 672 square feet, it was a small house, purchased by our parents before dad had joined the Navy. He had had little time to enjoy it, however, having died soon thereafter - a "war hero".

The house, with kitchen, living room, bathroom, two small bedrooms on the main level, and a full basement below, enabled Carol and me to both enjoy childhood adventures and to enact youthful indiscretions.

Against Mom's stern instructions, the blue rocking chair, positioned next to the living room window, often provided a wild, exciting opportunity for me to test the limits of gravity. Testing permanently ended one day after gravity won when I head-on crashed into the glass pane, creating both a spider-vein-shaped crack in the glass pane and a giant, purple knot on my forehead.

The kitchen also offered many life experiences.

It was a place where I much-too-frequently awoke, standing upright, having mistaken the kitchen floor for the bathroom toilet, leaving a pool of sleepwalk pee. Ugh!

In the kitchen, we learned that our failure to wash breakfast dishes timely found us eating that day's evening meal on the same plates — those with the dried remnants of the morning's fried egg breakfast. Though we saw no need to wash "dirties" until all the "cleans" had been used, Mom saw things differently and would give us an appropriate "Life Lesson."

Mom was not thrilled when she returned after work one afternoon to find Carol and I had painted the kitchen cabinets, table and chairs a "Chinese red". While we thought the red looked great with the gray walls, Mom was not happy — at all!

The kitchen was also the place Mom fed us pre-Vatican II, Friday night, salmon or tuna casserole. Ugh!

Bedrooms also offered "**Life Lessons**."

Because the top shelves of the two bedrooms were connected "tunnel-like," I could stealthily maneuver from the small bedroom to the large bedroom to spy on Carol and her girlfriends, Kay and Marie, whenever they experimented with fashion by trying on various pieces of lingerie. I enjoyed these "fashion shows" which provided me further education about girls and their anatomies. (I wonder if they knew of my presence.)

The basement provided wonderful experiences, also The floor was made of concrete, and with all items removed from the floor, it became a roller skating rink. Not bad — except when one skated into the floor drain and crashed into the nearby support pole. And when it rained, the rink and everything in it was inundated with water.

Because we lacked enough bedrooms on the main level, I several times tried to construct my bedroom in the basement. High humidity always doomed that effort.

Regrettably, dad's three boxes languished on that concrete floor, and, over time, they and their contents became mistreated, abused, and ruined.

1947 ff Brown High-Tops Mom continued to work to support her family. Nurses' wages were relatively low, but we scraped by. The house always suffered from deferred maintenance, but there was always enough food, often with the indulgence of the grocer across the street who kept an oft-used ledger of the funds we owed. The grocer even employed me periodically to sort soda bottles and stock shelves.

During these pre-teen into early teen years, we were visited by a series of male gift givers, from the Sears shoe salesman to the Omar man, to my barber to the antiques collector, to a criminal who was on parole. I suspect the gifts these visitors brought Carol and me were intended to enhance their opportunity to take advantage of a young widow — not particularly ingenious on their parts, but the gifts were still enjoyed by us.

Two of the "visitors" I recall most clearly —

> The Sears salesman, who offered us a ride home after meeting him when purchasing new brown, high-top shoes for me.
>
> The criminal out on parole, Paul H, whom we met when he delivered our dry cleaning.

And there were others, all of whom always initially expressed keen interest in the welfare of Mom's children and some of whom quickly proved a widely held belief that "all men are pigs."

It was also during these years that we had no automobile (mystery remains of what happened to dad's car after he enlisted). Clothes shopping required a trip downtown, which meant a six block walk to the bus stop, a likely 15 — 30 minutes wait for the bus, a 20 minute ride to downtown, and a reverse schedule to return home, hopefully having packages to carry.

We eagerly looked forward to the time we would have our own car.

As a child, I was "knock-kneed." The adult solution to correct this condition was to put me into brown, high-top shoes that did little more than provoke ridicule from my city peers. The only place Mom could find such shoes was the downtown Sears store. This particular store had a machine into which I could insert my feet and see an x-ray picture of my foot bones. Presumably, this helped me choose the right size shoes.

Our family shopping trips were not just for my ugly shoes. It was especially fun to go to the Younkers store and have lunch in "The Tea Room," where we could watch all the other people who had, mostly, also taken a bus to downtown to do their shopping. We all looked worn and frazzled but simultaneously happy to be there!

Carol liked to dine there to see the daily luncheon fashion show, as her only other exposure to fashion (other than the bedroom exchanges) was our mother's nursing uniforms and housecoats. These shopping trips broadened her exposure to mature fashion.

My ugly high-tops wore out quickly due to me dragging the toes on the ground when playing. At first, I liked the high-tops, as they were identical to those worn by Grampa Weaver and

Great Uncle Ben. I was proud to look like our farmer relatives. But after starting school in the city, wearing the high-tops came to be very embarrassing. My classmates wore low-tops with shoestrings — some even had low-top shoes without shoestrings! Life in the city can be very difficult for a kid in brown high-tops and bib overalls!

Our visits to Sears became often enough that the salesman recognized us and became too-well acquainted. "Mack" joined with Mom to convince me that I wouldn't have to wear this type shoe forever if I wore them while I was young, and they promised that wearing them while young was better than being a knock-kneed adult (another adult fable).

After shopping came the bus trip home. I would always run ahead to get a seat for us, but Mom would make me give up my seat for any elderly person who would otherwise have to stand. It didn't seem fair to me, as there were other boys my age who didn't give up their seats. But Mom told me I should practice good manners regardless of what the other boys do. Mom said dad always practiced good manners and, since I was the "man of the house" now, I should do the same. (She also told me the "man of the house" had to take out the garbage, do dishes and vacuum carpets. Those duties just made no sense to me at all!)

After a couple of times buying shoes from Mack, he offered us a ride home. Mom said my dad wouldn't like us accepting the offer, but the ride home in a car would be a blessing compared to the bus ride at the height of rush hour.

I was quite leery of having another man in the house. But Mack hung around and seemed to be a good companion to us, and his car provided opportunities to comfortably travel the city. Mom told Carol, I learned years later, she had become accustomed to being lonely after dad died, but she still felt desperate about the future. Acquaintances were becoming more distant, and she needed adult companionship regardless of what others might think.

In those days, all homeowners burned trash and garbage in a container in the yard or driveway. Mack suggested it might be good for me to watch each night's fire until it was fully extinguished, and he gave me a nickname I immediately hated — "Firewatcher". This "man of the house" didn't like being told what to do, especially by "Mack the Outsider". He also penned "Firewatcher" on the underside of the bill of my cap. My dislike for "Mack the Outsider" boiled!

I got revenge by throwing the Firewatcher cap into the burning trash, and I began a plot to "extinguish" Mack by undermining him whenever possible.

But Mack was writing his own ticket out of our lives. Mack's excessive enjoyment of beer soon demonstrated he was more interested in beer than in we three. He didn't mistreat us, but the beer dependence became obvious. I'm sure our neighbors were aware, also, as they often surreptitiously perused our trash. While we didn't socialize with the neighbors, I know they were concerned for our welfare.

After a fairly short time with us, and having experienced an increasingly unfriendly environment, "Mack the Outsider" simply exited our lives.

And I never bought another pair of brown high-tops!

1947 ff Catechism and Other Lessons Mom had a unique way of grilling us on our homework. If we were unable to provide a correct answer to her queries, she would shoot us with a rubber-tipped dart. Catholic catechism lessons, especially, got my full attention, so as to avoid those darts.

Mom also made sure we learned our manners. Open the door for the ladies. Provide appropriate protection by walking between a lady and the street. Assist a lady with her chair when seating. Hold a lady's coat when she is putting it on or taking it off. Chew your food with your mouth closed and swallow before taking another serving. Don't burp or fart in front of others. Eat neither garlic nor onions before a date (eating same at dinner with a date was ok if the date was eating likewise). And many more...

Through all the many lessons, Mom continued to struggle with depression and fatigue.

Curiously, other than when teaching us "manners," Mom never talked about our dad.

1947 ff Latchkey Kids During the school year and when we were not vacationing at the farm, we were "Latchkey Kids", providing us plenty of time to determine our own non-school activities.

A neighbor, Mrs. Hagman, usually stayed with us from 3:30 PM until Mom arrived home from work around 5:00 PM. Mrs. Hagman really was a very nice lady, but we totally disliked her because she severely restricted our freedom to self-determine our after school activities. She was very strict, always telling us what to do or not do. However, in time, she finally quit watching us, either because our obvious dislike of her drove her away or because Mom could no longer afford to pay her the two dollars per day. Or, Mom just decided she could trust us to behave as we grew older — or some combination of all the above.

And when mom's working hours became 3:00 PM to 11:00 PM, we were really free to self-determine in so many youthful ways. "3 to 11" became such magic hours!

1948 Job #1 Before the advent of shopping centers and Walmarts, every neighborhood was like a little village, where all neighbors were acquainted and looked out for each other. Each neighborhood contained only 2 or 3 blocks, and each had its own grocery store.

Grocery stores were small, and the owners were families who worked long hours stocking shelves, cutting meat, and keeping records. Many times the grocers would sell the groceries on credit, keeping a little record book for each customer, hoping that the customer could someday pay.

Our grocer was Mr. Joseph, and his store was immediately across the street from our 205 H. The store was arranged with shelves of canned goods across one side wall and in a center console that stood nearly 8 feet tall. On the other side wall were the checkout counter, cigarettes, pop, cash register, and candy. Produce was displayed under the front window and in back was the refrigerator and meat counter where Mr. Joseph cut orders as requested.

Like other grocery stores which expanded their offerings beyond groceries, Mr. Joseph began selling television sets. He and his wife's house was the nicest in the neighborhood, and they were the first to have a TV set. Perhaps they were just being nice to the neighbors, or perhaps it was informed marketing, but either way, it was great for us kids to be invited into their living room to watch TV. Each day's programs included high-quality kids' shows, like "Howdy Doody," "Captain Video," "The Mickey Mouse Show," the local "clown show," and the always mesmerizing "test pattern."

In due course, Mom bought our first TV from Mr. Joseph (on credit recorded in the little book). It was a top of the line "combination," with radio, phonograph, and a 12 inch screen. Mom paid $400, an enormous amount for us in 1950. What a treat, having one of the first TV sets in the neighborhood. Mr. Joseph later sold us an attachment that fit over the face of the screen and magnified the size to 16 inches — a giant technological leap forward!

Local legend claims that long before I ever considered needing a job, I helped myself to some of Mr. Joseph's fruit in his store. A peach, legend claims, was the booty. Legend further claims that Mom taught me a **"Life Lesson"** in honesty by making me take that peach back immediately, hand it directly to Mr. Joseph, admit that I had stolen it, and apologize.

My criminal activity did not prevent Mr. Joseph from giving me from my first paying job. For 10 cents an hour, **Job #1** consisted of sorting pop bottles (pop used to be sold in glass bottles that, when emptied, were returned to the bottling companies, where they were sanitized and reused), price-marking canned goods, and placing the cans in the proper spot on the shelves. Mr. Joseph probably calculated that, at 10 cents an hour, I could steal as many peaches as I wanted, and he would still come out ahead.

In time, Mr. Joseph did increase my pay and expanded my duties. In the end, I was making 15 cents an hour and waiting on customers (but he never let me operate the cash register or cut meat). Hmmm!

1948 Job #2
A city farmer, selling garden fresh strawberries door-to-door in our neighborhood, hired me, paying me 10 cents per pint I sold. Strawberries sold fast and easy, and it was a great job until the strawberry harvest was finished.

1948 Job #3
Unbeknown to Mom, I ordered a bulk of Christmas Cards, intending to sell them door-to-door. I quickly learned that Christmas cards are much harder to sell door-to-door than are strawberries.

Mom sent a record number of cards that year.

1948 Best Christmas Ever! Morning finally came, and under the tree were two brand new 26 inch Monarch bicycles — blue for Carol and red for me!

Out the door and into the snow I rode! Carol kept her bike indoor, spotlessly clean until spring.

1949 Job #4 I received my bulk order of Earl May garden seeds, intending to sell them door-to-door.

Mom planted a lot of seeds that spring.

1949 Dressed in White Perhaps the most important event in my life — First Holy Communion!

All the boys were dressed in white shirt, pants, and necktie, and the girls were in white dresses and headpieces. With all my classmates, it was a true moment of transition.

Thanks to all the nuns and priests who instructed, and brought us to, that special transition.

1949 Wish I Hadn't Said One day, I was having a difference of opinion with Mom. Not appreciating her position on whatever the issue was, I exclaimed: "You're crazy!" Mom's feelings were deeply hurt, and my shame became everlasting.

1949 Excited! Four weeks after I mailed the three box tops (from a breakfast cereal I did not even like), the Captain Video secret magic ring arrived! Boy, was I going to have fun with it!!

1949 ff Kay and Gregory R Carol and I were not the only latchkey kids in the neighborhood.

Siblings Kay and Gregory R attended the same grade school, All Saints Catholic, and were our same age.

Their mother was a saint, and their father tested her sainthood often. Their house was of similar quality to ours, but larger to accommodate their larger family. They had an older brother, Jerry, a much younger brother who, tragically, passed at age three when Kay was fourteen, and an even younger sister who was born when Kay was sixteen. A wonderful family, indeed!

My greatest attraction to their house was the backyard clubhouse built by Jerry. Many early life lessons were learned in that clubhouse in the darkness of night, as its excellent library of Sears Catalogues and Playboy magazines were quite educational, even by flashlight.

We did as much together as any brothers and sisters might do. We experimented with smoking. Kay and I practiced lip kissing (she was very good).

Among our other adventures, the four of us built a raft, from lumber scraps and tree limbs, and launched it into the Birdland Park Lagoon. Typical of our adventures, this adventure also ended in defeat, as our "Titanic" sank soon after launch. We emerged from the lagoon wet but safe - and thrilled.

1949 ff Don S — A lifetime Friend. I don't remember exactly when I met Don, but it was probably in kindergarten or first grade, after returning from our lengthy stay at Aunt Alma and Uncle Ben's farm.

Don's family, which included his parents and a sister, Carol Ann, lived a block and one-half from us.

Unlike our house, where Carol and I took turns sharing a small bedroom, Don always had his own bedroom. His sister's bedroom was located behind their parent's bedroom. Their kitchen had a small fold-down table, which served as their primary daily eating place. A small living room contained a larger dining table, a piano, a couch, and a TV. An enclosed porch and a basement completed the house, and in their backyard was a basketball hoop on a cool dirt court.

Also cool was their electric lawn mower, with rubber wheels and a very, very long power cord. Our steel mower was "sooo haarrdd" to push that it was infrequently used. But, on the plus side, we didn't need tape and tools to repair cut power cords. (Life is such a balancing act!)

Don's house was 804 sf & built in 1922 Our house was 672 sf and built in 1941.

Don was one of the smartest kids in class. We both played playground sports throughout grammar school and were in the cub scouts, boy scouts, and explorers together. We both played on the 8th grade basketball and baseball teams, which always finished in last place but whose teammates still thrilled our female classmates We both played street ball in the neighborhood and rode bicycles throughout the neighborhood and beyond.

Don was taller and stronger. He was the better athlete. On rare occasion, I found he was a better fist fighter, also. But, mostly we were close friends.

Being well-known in the neighborhood as a latchkey kid, I was often invited to eat at one of several neighbors' houses. Don's house was a frequent stop for dinner on school nights. Dinner might consist of a sandwich with only one piece of white bread, a few chips, and a glass of milk. These small meals probably explained the thin physiques of Don's family members. I always left hungry but quite appreciative!

Walking was very common in our neighborhood, as few families had two automobiles, and some, like ours, had none. Don's father needed their family car to get to his job across town in the very early morning hours. Don's mother worked in a downtown office, requiring a several block walk to/from the bus stop, as did Mom to get to her nursing job. Bicycling to/from grade school was normal for Don and me. Don was the first to see my new bike the day I purchased it.

Never in doubt, we eventually conquered grade school and advanced to high school together.

1949 ff My Beloved Twins There was another outstanding acquaintanceship developed on the first day of first grade at All Saints Catholic grade school, i.e., the "Twins."

Of course, they are actually known by their names — Barbara Ann and Beverly Ann. Blonde, blue-eyed, skinny, fun loving and delightful beauties, the twins stole my heart in first grade and never returned it. (Luckily, I was born with several hearts, few of which were ever returned.)

Barbara wore gold, narrow-rimmed glasses, which only added to her beauty. Though she didn't need them, Beverly would sometimes wear her sister's glasses, so I wouldn't know which twin I was pursuing at the moment. And I pursued them both all through grade school and would have been thrilled to have caught either.

A special memory is of the Valentine's Day party at their house. Slightly larger than our family's 205 H Avenue, and much better maintained, all classmates were invited, regardless of where they graded on my very immature "1 – 10 desirability" scale.

Following the exchange of Valentine cards, games were played. Especially exciting was "Spin the Bottle," played after adult supervisors exited. The spinner and the classmate to whom the mouth of the glass milk bottle pointed at the end of a spin were to go into the adjoining furnace room and, privately of course, lip kiss. An embrace was not required).

I intended my spin to stop when it pointed at a "10" (hopefully a twin), but, horridly, it pointed instead to a "2". Amid the laughter and giggles, "2" and I proceeded to the furnace room, closed the door, and stood there — rigidly apart. Our nine-year-old selves could not proceed, whether out of fear or lack of knowledge, I'm not sure. Or, perhaps the "2" graded me a "1" and didn't wish to be so associated. In any event, she and I finally agreed to exit the furnace room and falsely announce we had, indeed, claimed the game's reward. There were cheers and more giggles from all.

In our middle grade school years, I made a tin finger ring and, as a sign of my true love, presented it to one of the twins. I'm not sure which twin it was, as like the tides, true love switched in and out periodically as feelings changed. They would then pass the ring between them, leaving me confused as to which twin I was pursuing at the moment. The last to have it would have surely become my forever true love. However, the ring mysteriously disappeared eventually, and true love was lost forever. Darn!

Being left to otherwise demonstrate my true love commitment, I carved the initials "BA" into the back of my left hand. I felt such joyful pain, standing at the bathroom sink, as I cut my skin with the point of a scissors. Pouring black ink into the cuts was intended to make it a permanent tattoo. Fortunately, the inking process failed to become permanent. But, just like the tin ring, the initials "BA", while they lasted, dramatically demonstrated my love for them.

Sometime during our later grade school years, the twins' mother passed. Since our mother was still an unmarried widow, Carol and I thought there could be a perfect union between our families. (The twins also had an handsome brother, Jimmy, with whom Carol was smitten.) However, the union failed to initiate.

Thus, I was left to serve my infatuation with "My Beloved Twins" from my nighttime viewing spot, hidden under a house mover's timbers, across the alley from their bedroom window. An understanding of how a house mover stacks those huge timbers, used for moving very heavy houses, would enable the reader to realize how truly dangerous crawling within them was for me. But, I was a lad smitten by two fair maidens, so the risk seemed certainly worth the reward.

Unfortunately, although "under-the-timbers" efforts were attempted several times during the grade school years, just like so many of my similar "educational" efforts (e.g., our neighbor's daughter's bedroom window was directly across from mine), success was minimal. I finally realized the risks had exceeded the rewards. But much like golf, don't you know, one good shot, and you go back for more.

1949 Job #5 Mr. Costanzo hired me for his corner grocery. He started me in the returned bottle basement (I had gained substantial experience at Mr. Joseph's store) and eventually assigned me to the cashier's counter. Terminated soon thereafter, perhaps because he suspected me of stealing cigarettes (which I did not do), Mr. Costanzo simply said I wasn't needed any longer. Curiously, another neighborhood boy was soon sorting returned bottles and working the cashier's counter.

1950 Monday Morning Inquisition Paramount among the early grade school years' rules was required attendance at Sunday mass. We were destined to everlasting pain & suffering in HELL if we missed Sunday mass.

Every Monday morning at All Saints School, the nuns would ask: "Who did not attend Sunday mass at All Saints Church yesterday?" Believing that the eventual reward for lying was eternal damnation, we would not dare to deny our failure of faithful attendance. And it wasn't just failure to attend Sunday mass anywhere; it was failure to attend at our home parish. (I later began to skeptically believe that that particular rule may have emanated from the church's Sunday monetary offerings collections process).

Those of us who admitted to the Sunday mass transgression were directed to leave class and go to the back pews of the church to discuss our failures with Father (later Monsignor) Maher, a hulk of an Irishman who, on Monday mornings, was terror personified. Father would interrogate each transgressor about the reason for missing mass. Some of us were legitimately sick, some unconvincingly claimed illness, some attended elsewhere (doubtful), and then there were Carol & me. Unable to construct a believable reason for missing mass, and fearful of going straight to hell for both missing mass and then lying about it, we would truthfully admit to sleeping late and not being adequately motivated.

After a deafening, teeth-rattling reprimand, Father's next question would address our mother's failure to bring us to mass, creating yet another challenge to my search for eternal salvation. Again, the nun's strict teachings led us to be fearful, and we had to admit Mom was also sleeping in. More reprimand would follow, including a strong suggestion that Mom should journey to the parish house and visit with Father about our choices in life.

These frequent Monday morning meetings with Father Maher also taught me one of **life's lessons**, i.e., whom you know does matter. Some of those classmates frequently with us on Monday mornings were from families whose parents provided social interaction, and, I suspect, strong financial support, for the parish (more skepticism?). To those classmates, his admonition was simple: "You don't belong here, and you may now leave". Why, I wondered, did he wait to tell them to leave until the rest of us sinners fully embarrassed ourselves with our flimsy excuses and revealing truths?

Of course, confession followed, and all was forgiven — at least, until the next Monday morning.

(Carol soon realized a new **life lesson** from these Monday morning interrogations, i.e., too much honesty may be disadvantageous. She simply quit admitting to missing mass. Problem solved!)

1950 Tragedy A young neighborhood boy was struck and killed on the street in front of our house. We had experienced losing a dog to a car at the same place previously, but this was different. I hoped to never see a dead person again.

1950 Car Rides Several other families in our neighborhood were without an automobile. So, it was exciting for all neighbors when someone came home with a new (or new/used) car. Such was the case in 1950, when Mom drove home in her brand new, 1950 Ford, 2-door sedan. The neighbors flocked to inspect the car. With only six cylinders , no overdrive, and black wall tires, it had no luxuries. But it was ours, and we were thrilled.

The car also facilitated Mom's quest to be a comedian. More than once, when pestered by Carol and me to go for a car ride, she would tell us to get properly dressed and get in the car, and she would then drive directly into the garage, laughing hysterically! Ride over!

1951 Stern Warning In fifth grade, after another bout of fisticuffs with a particular classmate, his mother visited our house to discuss the matter. Fortunately, I was alone at home and did not invite her in. Unfortunately, as she departed, I demonstrated my newly learned method of communication, and I offered her a middle-finger salute

The following day at school, Sister Paula invited me into her "special" room and showed me her arsenal containing all sorts of disciplinary tools, including a baseball bat, rulers of various sizes and weights, and what I believed to be "steel knuckles."

Suggesting I change my course of life, and apologize to the boy's mother, Sister Paula released me to my mother for further discussion.

1951 Wish I Hadn't Said Our 205 H yard flourished with several fruit trees and grape vines. Annually, Grandmother Neva (actually, step-grandmother, as Mom's mother had passed before Carol and I were born), would come to our house with Grandfather Weaver and harvest the peaches. The peaches were lush and sweet, and she would take them home for canning. One day, not even close to harvest time (keep in mind she and Weaver frequently invited Carol and me to stay on the farm and treated us very well, including baking the most wonderful Angel Food cake for our enjoyment), for some unknown reason, I felt compelled to tell Neva: "You can't have our peaches anymore!" Her feelings were greatly hurt, and I never got to taste her Angel Food cake again!

1952 ff Carol Our developing tastes in music were opposites, with Carol preferring country and me preferring big band and jazz. When home alone together, we often argued about radio station choices. The choice was often decided with a physical encounter.

Though always mobile, Carol endured significant back pain. When in sixth grade, a doctor recommended she wear a full body cast to help straighten her spine and reduce pain. Cast from shoulders to hips, with a circular cutout in front accommodating belly motion, she was unable to wear normal, contemporary clothing. Instead, she wore a "muumuu", which was much like a full length robe. The cast and the robe subjected her to many taunts and jeers from schoolmates, especially the boys. Daily life in such circumstances was humiliating for Carol and, undoubtedly, caused permanent emotional distress.

The cast also caused constant discomfort. Carol would push a long wire hanger inside the cast to scratch every itch. Personal hygiene was a challenge. After months of trying, she begged me to help cut off the cast, which we did successfully. But for all the pain and suffering she endured, the months spent wearing the body cast did not alleviate her back pain. With the doctor firmly believing casting would eventually produce results, Carol was once again placed in a full body cast for several months, only to again endure taunting but, again, without pain alleviation. The pain was chronic, varying in intensity from day-to-day. The body casting solution was permanently discarded after the second try.

Though I do not believe our physical encounters were the original source of her back pain, I greatly regret those occasional encounters we had about music choices on the radio, as they may have caused her some pain, also.

1953 ff Serving Mass I came late to Server training. Starting in fifth grade, all male students at All Saints Catholic School were required to serve mass. Training was directed by a stern Sister Paula, an unmerciful Sister of Mercy. Included in the training was properly laying out the priest's vestments, learning all the Latin recitations, ensuring the water and wine were ready, holding the paten while serving communion, ringing the bells at the correct times, etc.

Unless the vestments were laid out in proper order, the always hurried priest could not quickly put them on. I was supposed to understand the significance of each garment, which would help me put them in proper order (layered with the outside garment on the bottom to the inside garment on the top), but I just never got them right, giving the priest yet another reason to scold me. Fortunately, when Don was also serving that day, he would correct my errors and save me a scolding.

I never got all the Latin responses right, either. I would mumble them while Don would shout them out precisely, thankfully covering my mumbles.

I had no problem handling the water and wine and could always get them placed properly.

And sometimes I rang the bells at the wrong time (Sister Paula believed I did that purposely).

Assisting the priest (usually Father Maher) at the communion rail was always a challenge. He would serve communion to each communicant's mouth while moving along the rail, while the server would precede him along the rail, walking backwards in order to place the paten under the chin of each communicant, catching any host that might be dropped. Challenges included not tripping on my long cassock and not being stepped on by Father while moving too slowly.

Another challenge for me was arriving at church on time. Not only was it embarrassing to walk into the sanctuary after mass had already started, but I knew another priestly lecture, about how I had offended God, was forthcoming after mass. I soon knew that lecture by heart. Sorry, God!

While Sister Paula didn't consider me an accomplished mass server, she was so short of servers, I survived her wrath and continued to be assigned serving duties.

“Thanks!” are certainly due to Don for his assistance on yet another important part of my growth and development.

Sorry for my failures, Father and Sister!

1953 Oh! My! Goodness!!! So this is what they mean by “puberty”!

1953 Wish I Hadn’t Said As a twelve year-old Boy Scout, I enjoyed frequent camping trips with other Boy Scouts. And like all kids that age, I often tested various “don’t do that” parental instructions. On this night, we were testing the oft-stated “…you may not smoke…” admonition.

Another Boy Scout had brought a pack of cigarettes. Five of us sat in a circle inside a tent (after lights-out, illuminated with only a flashlight), the pack was opened, and a cigarette was lit. The cigarette was then passed around for each of us to take a drag. When it came to me, the end was very wet. Demonstrating my profound ignorance, I exclaimed: “Who lipped this?” Sadly, the responsible scout was an African-American, who until then had been a good friend of mine. Not only did I choke on the inhaled smoke, I also lost that good friend.

1953 Vows Taken It had dawned on me that the only meaningful goal of earthly life is to attain eternal life. Such is truly my greatest awareness!

It came after Confirmation, when the Bishop named me Michael, slapped me on the cheek, and proclaimed me a "Soldier of Christ."

I personally vowed to achieve that goal.

At the end of the sacramental ceremony, the Bishop also required a vow from each new soldier to never drink alcohol until at least the age of 21—also a worthy goal.

1953 Nights in a 1935 Ford One of my all-time favorite automobiles is a 1935 Ford convertible. In our neighborhood, Ted, an admirable 18 year-old, owned one. Being only 12 years old at the time, why Ted would allow Gregory R and me to ride with him on many summer nights remains a mystery, but it was a period of maturation and excitement for all of us.

Maturing comes from new experiences. Sitting in the back seat of this old convertible was an exhilarating and educational experience, as Ted and his friend John, both being older and wiser, instructed us about girls, smoking, and beverages. Occasional beers may have been consumed by Ted and John, but I did not participate due to my confirmation vow (a vow strictly kept until college).

On our late night journeys around town, Greg and I would jump into the back seat of the Ford, John would ride shotgun, we would light our Lucky Strikes, and off into the night we would roar, seeking yet another young men’s maturing adventure.

The Ford was 18 years old — much past its "use by" date. With "three speeds on the floor," the ragged top flapping in the breeze, the transmission groaning, and the engine whining, we could cover most of the town during each evening's journey, occasionally venturing "close to the sun" at the hands of another car full of similar after-dark adventurers or of a menacing youth group loitering on a street corner. Fortunately, our escapes from danger were always without injury.

Our evening adventures lasted for only a few weeks, ending, I suspect, when someone's mother discovered, and disagreed with, how we were obtaining our educations. Or, perhaps, Ted and John found better ways to spend their evenings. But the exhilarating evening adventures did finally come to an end, requiring Greg and me to seek maturation experiences elsewhere — which never seemed to be a problem.

For the very inexpensive, invaluable education gained while in that four-wheeled classroom, we surely owe a debt of gratitude to the great Henry Ford!

1953 Ronnie — A Lifetime Friend We first became acquainted while living in the same neighborhood but attending different schools— he at public and me at Catholic. We played neighborhood football games in the street near his house. He was a strong and rough player, I soon discovered, and I always tried to be on his team.

Though Ronnie had little interest for school, he was quite smart and had other interests. His bedroom, located on the enclosed front porch of their small, one-bedroom house, was filled with interesting things, including gerbils, maps, telescopes, science and magic tricks.

He became interested in homing pigeons and built pigeon cages on the side of the family garage. With his help, I soon had my own homing pigeons in cages attached to the back side of our 205 H garage. His pigeons seemed to prosper, while mine usually contracted some mysterious illness and soon passed. Mom and our neighbors were relieved at each passing, as they always worried about disease being spread by those "filthy" pigeons.

Ronnie's family had a dog, Cookie, and she was certainly an important part of their family. When Cookie died, Ronnie's family decided to conduct her funeral in their back yard between a huge tree and their garage. Because they knew I was (by then) a "go-to-church-every-Sunday Catholic", they asked me to say a few words over Cookie. However, being a "go-to-church-every-Sunday Catholic", I was sure I would burn in the fires of hell for praying for the non-human soul of a dog, so after I stood silent for too long, they said their own words, and Cookie got a heartfelt send off from the family.

Ronnie's mother, Dorothy, was quite attractive, in a "Playboy Playmate" kind of way, which may have caused Ronnie some angst when she would sunbathe in the backyard in full view of the very appreciative men and boys of the neighborhood. Not limiting her sun worshiping to the backyard, when Ronnie and his mom picked me up from my grandparent's farm one summer day, they arrived in her big, gray Packard convertible — with the top down, of course, enabling her to enjoy the mobile sunbathing opportunity — wearing a most revealing personal "top". Grandmother Neva was less impressed than was Grandfather Weaver, another appreciative observer!

Ronnie's father, Don, was a debonair, outgoing man with a well-coifed mustache. No doubt, he featured himself as a lady's man, and he probably was. He earned a living in various manners, most involving his well-honed skills as a mechanic. There wasn't any mechanical challenge he couldn't handle. Also a pilot, he owned a Pitcairn bi-plane, with which he towed advertising banner, and a small Cessna. Don restored several antique motorcycles, including a four-cylinder Indian (vintage 1936), which he rode daily to work. The restorations were better than new. Generous with his time, he helped me whenever I needed a mechanic's skills to solve a problem — which was often.

These were two very fine people, Don and Dorothy, who treated me exceptionally well.

1953 Interior Decorating It was not unusual for the neighbors to see when "new" furniture arrived at our house. Once, when Ronnie's folks were discarding an old, worn couch, Ronnie and I (proudly) carried that old couch two blocks, during daylight, from his house to mine, replacing the really old, worn and torn couch in our living room.

At another time, when Ronnie's folks were replacing a worn carpet, Ronnie and I (proudly) retrieved it from the dumpster and installed it in my family's living room, thus adding more glamour to our house.

Ronnie's folks appreciated the free removals, and our family appreciated the bright "new" interior touches.

And the public transporting during daytime gave our always curious neighbors something else to talk about.

1953 Job #6 I delivered weekday and Sunday newspapers for three summer months. On my route, there were many short-term rental properties whose occupants neglected to pay their paperboy before they moved away. Many paperboy alums say delivering papers is a great experience, but mine was a horrible job. Sunday mornings were especially awful, arising early and delivering those very heavy Sunday newspapers. Mom always helped cheerfully, and I'm sure she celebrated quietly when I retired my newspaper carrier's bag.

1953 Birdland On a hot summer day, what would a city kid like more than to spend hours at the swimming pool. Our closest public swimming pool was "Birdland". I don't know how it got that name, as there were neither a great number of common birds nor a small number of uncommon birds, nor was it a jazz haven, but everyone knew where you were going when you said: "Birdland!"

Birdland was more than a place to find respite from the heat of the sun. It was a place of excitement for kids growing up — a place for recreation and education. Kids would learn a lot about life, the characters in life, and themselves.

Pretty, well-endowed, young girls would strut past gawking young boys, fully anticipating being pushed into the water while screaming "bloody murder", as if surprised. The less demonstrative girls would prefer to maintain as much privacy as possible by avoiding the boys and/or by wrapping large beach towels strategically around their bodies, while still getting their sun tans.

I relished Birdland's activities until the time I stealthily pushed a very proudly endowed, strutting, and then protesting, Karen, into the deep water, only to be surprised to learn from her screams that she really could not swim. Her screaming jolted the deeply tanned lifeguards off their perches and, fortunately, all ended well, although I found it necessary to become quite scarce around Birdland for some time thereafter.

Birdland was also a place the muscularly endowed young men and boys could display their bodies — something I was not prepared to do. Not only was I not naturally endowed with Charles Atlas muscles, I was not cool like the muscular boys who would recline on towels, with their tanning oil gleaming and cigarettes smoking. Nor could I compete with their diving skills.

Birdland had 3, 5, 12, 24, and 33 foot high boards from which to demonstrate one's diving skills. Having succeeded in jumping from 12 feet, I climbed to the 24 foot board. It was then I suddenly realized 24 feet was really, really high — and well beyond my skill level. Embarrassed, I bashfully climbed down to the 12 foot board — slipping past the up-climbing, deeply tanned, cool boys as they ascended to 33 feet — and I successfully jumped — meekly — feet first!

If one ever wished to observe the anatomies of well-endowed men, Birdland's men's shower was the place. Birdland's rules required swimmers to bathe sans swimsuit both before entering the pool and upon leaving. For the modest and shy, that was a rule most often ignored. But for those egotistic, male god's of summer, it provided an opportunity to shine -- and to simultaneously embarrass the rest of us mere mortals.

Had we known who he was, we would have generously thanked the architect of Birdland's building. He designed the roof with openings above the shower areas — on both the boys' and the girls' sides of the building. Rules prohibited climbing onto the roof, but that didn't stop the adventurous. When pool management was absent, an inconspicuous stroll pass the girls' roof opening was essential and educational — not that I ever did it, but one could, if one was so inclined.

"No urinating in the pool" was another Birdland rule ignored by many boys and, I expect, by many girls, especially after learning that the urine did not really change the color of the pool water surrounding the urinator. In hindsight, I've wondered, what was it in the water that tasted so bitter and caused such redness in our eyes?

A day at Birdland was quite a treat for only 10 cents. It was even better if, after a day of swimming, pushing, jumping, urinating, and observing, a 25-cent Birdland hot dog with mustard would cap the day! Such was the case one hot summer day when I didn't have the needed 25 cents, but a new social contact offered to fund my post-swim feast. Little did I know my benefactor would have a long-term impact on my family's life.

That was the day I met James Eugene, my future stepfather, "pro tem."

1953 Stepfather After treating us to two of Birdland's fantastic 25-cent hotdogs with mustard, James Eugene (aka Jim) and his Marine Corps buddy, Ed, accompanied Carol and me to our house. I neither recalled seeing the marines in the pool nor did I recall an invitation to our home being offered but, supposedly coincidentally, there we all were in Harry and Lorene's 205 H Avenue home.

Being so young at the time .I was easily impressed by anyone, especially heroes like these two strong, young, fighting machines, who had bought me fantastic 25-cent hot dogs. Ooh rah!

Mom and Carol were already acquainted with Sargent Jim and Corporal Ed, so the coincidental meeting at the pool may not have been so coincidental at all. Mom and Carol had met Jim previously at a small café where he worked the counter while on leave from active duty. Why Jim was in town, I don't know, as he had no known attachment here. Ed must have been simply a tag-along, and he was soon just a distant and forgotten memory. Regardless, that day was the beginning of a relationship that had many more positives for me than for Mom and Carol.

How assumptions can be wrong! I thought Jim was interested in Carol, but he was really interested in Mom (of course, as she was a beautiful lady). Jim was 22 and Mom was 38. Love blossomed. Ed might have been interested in Carol, but he left. Jim stayed. And stayed. And stayed. He stayed so long, he overstayed his leave and became AWOL from the Corps.

After receiving several visits to our house by Navy MPs who were searching for their awol sergeant, and thinking his luck was running out, Mom decided to use her vacation to return Jim to his base in San Diego. We all climbed into our non-air-conditioned, green, six-cylinder, 1950 2-door Ford with blackwall tires and no overdrive sedan the next morning and headed post haste past the cornfields of Iowa, across the plains of Nebraska, through the Colorado mountains, into the Nevada desert, and eventually into the promised land (California, of course), taking Jim to the Navy depot, where he reported for duty and begged forgiveness.

Crossing the desert with the canvas bag of water hanging on the front bumper was an uncomfortable experience shared by many other common folk in those days. But there were plenty of diversions from the discomfort.

We stayed overnight with Uncle Ray and Aunt Beulah in Las Vegas, where I was fascinated that their back yard's beautiful green grass touched the beginning of what appeared to be an endless, barren desert.

Our car windows became covered with decals, evidencing the many enchanting places we visited. In those days, the more decals on the car windows, the more impressed were neighbors when vacationers returned home. We saw real Indians and Indian teepees, real cowboys and cowboy horses, a painted desert, a man with two heads, and lots of silver jewelry. Route 66 was a hoot!

We deposited Jim at the San Diego NAVY depot gate and headed back across the desert to home. On this long and dreary trip back, the canvas bag on the front bumper provided water mostly for cooling Mom's weary feet, leaving us quite thirsty between gas stops.

Upon arrival home, our friends enjoyed our explanations of each of the window stickers.

Jim spent time in the brig, lost his stripes, and was soon deployed to Korea.

1953 Job #7 Grandfather Weaver thought this would be a good learning experience for me. Called "walking the beans," we walked the field between the soy bean plant rows, using a sickle or a knife, cutting down the remaining corn stalks and weeds which had survived prior attempted assignations with chemicals and/or cultivation. Pay was poor and fingers got bloody from handling that very sharp sickle. A two-day learning experience was more than enough for me.

1954 "Good Feed" Feeling As a child without a father to teach and encourage me in sports, I was not accomplished at any of the usual sports, such as basketball, baseball, and football. It was discouraging to always be chosen last for a team.

As such, it was a great feeling when, as a seventh grader playing basketball on the school court at recess, I was praised with a "Good feed!" acclamation after I skillfully passed the basketball to an eighth-grade teammate, a very skilled basketball player, who drove for the winning basket. I remember nothing else about that game, except I finally won some praise for a good play.

Feb 1955 Ad Altare Dei In keeping with the Boy Scout promise ("On my honor, I will do my best to do my duty to God…") and the Scout law ("A Scout is reverent…"), and for doing 200 hours of service for my church, and along with my other classmate scouts, I received the Ad Altare Dei award.

We wore the award, bronze crosses suspended from a ribbon of Papal and national colors, proudly.

1955 Wow! It finally arrived! Two weeks after I mailed the request, the Rosemary Clooney pinup pic finally arrived. Boy, am I going to have fun with this!!

1955 Stepfather In the 18 months he was away on military duty, he never saw combat action, but the pictures we received showed him standing in a U.S. marine campsite on top of a bleak, cold, Korea mountain-top. On the plus side of his "vacation in paradise," he did get some GI R&R in a relatively nice Korea city, from which he sent us "oriental" jackets, a silverware set, and a very nice china set.

Upon completion of his military duty, Jim returned to our little 205 house — and moved in. A Justice of the Peace presided at their wedding. Jim wore a blue sport coat with a white boutonniere. Mom wore a nice dress from the closet (she had few from which to choose). A small, white wedding cake, with plastic bride and groom atop, was sliced and served. Jim's favorite dessert, a Reed's double nutty fudge sundae and a 16 ounce Pepsi, were enjoyed. Though invited, no relatives attended. And that was just it.

Distressed, I was no longer "man of the house."

So then, our "modern family" of four consisted of a teenage boy, a teenage girl, and a presumably happy mother and stepfather (whom many considered to be much too close in age to his stepchildren, having been born in 1931) living in a 672 square foot, 2-bedroom house. It was rightly decided Carol would have sole use of the second bedroom, giving me the living room couch for a bed. That arrangement was the best we could do, given the circumstances.

Like our relatives, our neighbors were generally not supportive of our "modern family" concept, either. Looking at it from the neighbors perspective, we did give them many reasons to hope we would move, like the rusty and broken, but periodically driven, 1950 Mercury sedan parked on our front lawn, and the many friends' motorcycles lacking mufflers as they roared away at any time of the day or night.

Jim enjoyed various blue collar jobs and tried to be a good provider. He framed houses for a while, even on frigid winter days, providing rather unsteady employment. He later became a welder at a manufacturing plant, where he soon became a union steward, a position which provided more steady employment than just being a welder. Mom continued in her nursing career, and Carol and I continued our growing and maturing experiences.

Jim tried to fill the father role for us. Carol would have none of that relationship, and they did not get along well. She met his rules with great resistance. It was difficult for him, being a relatively young stepfather from an authoritarian, blue collar background, to deal with a stepdaughter who had her own ideas of self-determination. His parenting skills were not well-developed, and she had a mind of her own.

On the other hand, I fared much better with Jim, though I was blind to the dysfunction in our family. He was more like a big brother to me. Jim helped coach my grade school baseball team and volunteered with the Boy Scout troop on camping trips. An example of his parenting skills was, while driving us on an in-town errand, informing Gregory R and me that doing certain "things" would cause hair to grow on the palms of one's hands. Thereafter, Gregory and I were always alert for kids with hairy palms.

Interestingly, Mom and Jim appeared to complement each other well. I never heard raised voices or disagreements of any type between them. Could it be they were actually happy together?

I know little about Jim's background and education. I'd guess he completed high school or earned a GED diploma along the way. He never mentioned his parents or his hometown, but he claimed Pennsylvania Dutch heritage. Other than his brother, whom we once visited in Gary, Indiana, Jim mentioned no family. He was a pack-a-day smoker, favoring non-filtered Camel cigarettes, thus providing another great source of "butts" for me and an occasional "freshie" unsmoked prize when he wasn't looking.

Jim was not a drinker. However, he was addicted to Reed's double nutty fudge sundaes and 16-ounce Pepsi Colas — his almost daily treats!

Jim enjoyed hunting and fishing, which I did not enjoy, so he often took other neighborhood boys with him for those activities. He would return home with his prizes and prepare them for our dinners. I avoided dinners those nights (does anyone truly enjoy "carp stew" or lead-laden baked rabbit?)

1955 Eighth Grade Dance We had our eighth grade dance today. I danced with Don.

Early in the school year, some enlightened parents had determined we students needed to develop our "advanced" social graces. To wit, we started taking ballroom dancing classes.

Each Saturday morning, Don, I and others would arrive at the dance studio at 10:00 AM to learn, and practice, those challenging dance steps. The only dance in which I achieved a minimum degree of expertise was the fox trot — left, right, left; left, right, left; left, right, left — repeating ad nauseam — always in a straight line to the end of the dance floor, turn left towards the wall at the next end of the dance floor, turn left towards the wall at the next end of the dance floor, left again toward the wall at the point of beginning, turn left and do it again until the music stopped. Pure agony!

(Did I mention the one redeeming feature of dance class that brought us back Saturday after Saturday, i.e., the outstanding quality of one of the instructors, a well-endowed young lady of our same age?)

Not realizing it when we began taking lessons, a school dance was planned at the end of the school year to celebrate the successful completion of our achievements. So, there we were in the All Saints School basement for the eighth grade school dance — the entire class of 20 boys and girls plus chaperones. The music began, and we were instructed to find a dance partner. Timid as I was, especially around the girls, I searched for and found my best dance partner — Don. Fortunately, like the dance studio, the basement room was also square, having four walls, with four pillars located near the center of the room, and we danced wall-to-wall and around the pillars. What a magical night! Loosely embracing, I danced forward while Don danced backwards, so I guess that meant I was the guy, and he was the girl.

I suspect Don will deny this story, but it is absolutely factual!

1955 ff Carol Carol had her boyfriends. Her first serious relationship was with Charles, a farm boy several years older than she. I don't know how they met, but Charles would pick her up after work (he worked in an agricultural chemicals processing plant in town) in his yellow, two-door, late-model Pontiac, with the fragrance-tree hanging from the rear view mirror. They would be gone for hours, riding around within and outside the city. Occasionally, little brother me would be allowed to ride along.

Charles always smelled of Old Spice — lots of Old Spice! Carol was 15 years old at that time, much too young to be out riding around with an older gentleman.

Carol and Charles continued their relationship for several months, but it ended rather tragically when Charles fell into a vat of boiling chemicals at the agricultural processing plant. A shame, as he was probably the best, nicest, and most gracious man Carol ever loved.

Carol attended (sporadically) public high school, but she found school to be of insufficient interest to pursue formal education aggressively. When being dropped off in front of her high school, she and a girlfriend would often fake entering the school and, instead, would veer off elsewhere for the day. She dropped out after her sophomore year.

Through these years at home, Carol and stepfather Jim were in constant conflict. Giving him the benefit of the doubt, Jim may have felt Carol was on a negative path, and he was honestly, but incapably, trying to re-direct her to a better future. Or, perhaps Jim's parental efforts contributed to Carol's drifting further away.

1956 6th Avenue Predator's Playground Hitchhiking was a common way to get around town for male teenagers, including at day's end of high school classes. The streets would virtually fill with students seeking a ride to home or their part-time jobs. Boys' hitching was of no great concern for parents, as there were never reports of assaults then — by either the hitchers or the drivers who picked them up — and never, of course, was hitching a concern of the indestructible teenagers.

My usual route, when heading home, was north on 6th avenue. I would arrive after school as quickly as possible to get a good spot where drivers could easily pull over to the curb, out of the traffic flow, to safely complete the pickup. Often, there would be at least two of us hitching together, but never more than two, as drivers would usually not pick up more than two at a time. Perhaps drivers felt more than two was dangerous. And since most local drivers knew the Catholic high school students were safe to pick up, rides came easy.

I was 15 years of age on this particular day when a driver pulled over, and I hopped in. The driver seemed vaguely familiar — a pudgy, balding man in his late 50's, I estimated. After having driven a few blocks, sharing some meaningless conversation about where I went to school, my grade, what sports I liked, etc., "pudgy" reached across the front seat and grabbed my crotch.

Suddenly, I remembered his face as that of the man who had done the same thing to me years earlier, when I was 11. That time, I managed to bail out of the car at a stoplight and simply ran away. But this time, I gifted him a bloody nose, shouted him appropriate names, and quickly bailed out of his car.

I never mentioned these incidents to my mother, for fear of heightening her ceaseless concerns about things that could happen to her latchkey kid (such as her fear that prevented me from playing high school football). Still, those incidents did not change my reliance on hitching.

Although "pudgy" has likely achieved his appropriate eternal reward, unfortunately, others like him continue to menace their own 6th Avenue playgrounds.

1956 Neighborhood Excitement I arrived home one evening from a church meeting to the sight of flashing squad car lights and a crowd in front of 205 H. Paul H, quite inebriated, had arrived earlier and, with pistol in hand and pointed, threatened to harm Jim.

The neighbors were not pleased with such excitement.

We never heard from or about Paul thereafter.

1956 Road Rams Years before I met Ronnie, I had seen farmer/neighbor Harold come speeding into Grandfather Weaver's graveled lane, followed by a cloud of dust, with loud exhausts announcing his arrival. That marked the beginning of my lifelong fascination with motorcycles.

Harold didn't give me a ride that day, but I still remember how much fun he was having as he revved the engine on that old Indian motorcycle and sped off down the country road.

The same year, I soon noticed blonde-haired, twin boys speeding around our city neighborhood on their identical green motorbikes. They were also having the greatest time of their young lives, and I wanted the same. I became obsessed. I wanted to have my own motorbike, but I was "… much too young, and they are dangerous!" said Mom. Begging was fruitless, leaving me to ride the green machines only in my dreams.

Then one day, Ronnie exited his garage on his Doodle Bug, and my life took a new direction.

Ronnie was the first kid in the neighborhood to acquire a Doodle Bug - a two-wheeler that had a Briggs and Stratton engine, two small wheels, handle bars, a seat, and a platform for the driver's feet. It achieved speeds of ten miles per hour on a good day.

Ronnie was always twiddling with the Bug to make it go faster — and then to repair whichever part broke. We neighborhood boys would stand in line to get a turn to drive the Bug. As I began to spend more time with Ronnie, working on his Bug or whatever other two-wheeler he had at the time, I was able to get more than my fair share of Bug rides. It wasn't long before I was planning to get my own Bug.

Though it wasn't a Bug, I did acquire a two-wheeler – a basket-case 125 cc Jawa. Since my mother would not allow me to own a motorcycle, I left it at Ronnie's house where he and I spent many evenings in his basement, rebuilding that bike and smoking cigarettes – two pleasures prohibited by Mom.

In time, Ronnie and I were spending most of our time around new friends' motorcycle garages, learning a lot about bikes and more of life. My academic progress suffered accordingly, and I lost interest in spending time on the family farm.

Bigger and better bikes were acquired by Ronnie. Even Ronnie's parents, Don and Dorothy, entered the world of crazies. Don began to ride and restore antique bikes. New friends were made through visits to Lynn's Motorcycle Shop, which was the unofficial headquarters of the Road Rams Motorcycle Club. We were soon all members of the club, wearing black leather jackets, emblazoned in silver on their backs with an awesome looking Ram with huge head and horns. Dorothy and another rider's wife were always fashionably attired in white leather jackets, pants, boots, and helmets. I would ride dual with Ronnie. No doubt neighbors thought a two-wheeled circus had come to town as we rode out for the Rams' Friday night festivities!

Don and Dorothy would often invite me to join them and Ronnie as a guest for dinner at their favorite restaurant before meeting with the other Rams. I always looked forward to those invitations but with mixed feelings, as too often at those dinners, they would tell Ronnie "…you should be more like Michael."

Statements like that, coming from his parents, were hard on him, making him angry and absent from me for several days, leaving me without a ride. I still don't know why his parents wanted him to be more like me, although his stuttering, eating with his mouth open, pimpled complexion, and sub-par school grades may have been causal. Both Ronnie and I hated these parental critiques.

Ronnie's anger at the comparison likely led to the one time he and I entered into a fisticuffs match (another one of the reasons I gave up fisticuffs). Ronnie was bigger and stronger, and I would be the recipient of all the bumps and bruises that day, as well as again losing my dual ride with him for an extended period of time.

Back to Friday nights, after dinner, we would assemble with the other "Rams" at Lynn's for the evening's event. Often, a poker run was played, taking participants all over the city, following the event planner's directional hints, searching for the hidden playing cards that would produce the winning poker hand. The event would usually terminate at a member's home for awards and non-alcoholic refreshments.

1957 Oops! On the way to school one beautiful morning, I introduced the rear fender of my stepfather's '50 Mercury sedan to a truck's front bumper while pulling into a gas station to illegally purchase cigarettes. Driver of the truck claimed it was my fault. Though I disagreed, all blame fell on me!

1957 Priestly Advice I had achieved good academic success my first year in high school, making the honor roll five of the six grading periods. Much of that success came from studying with Don at his house after school, until I became interested in motorcycles. But in sophomore year, my interest in academics waned, and I found ways to either not arrive at school in the morning or ways to leave early — in both cases, to pursue other fun but less meaningful activities, which usually found Ronnie and me pursuing some more two-wheeled excitement. Little time remained for homework.

A priest teacher, who keenly observed my academic progress was slowing, attempted to get me back on the high scholastic achievement track. Called to his office, he interrogated me as to why my interest in school was failing

Feeling uncomfortable with his questioning, I offered the same excuse I had used many times before to explain any of my failures — "I don't have a father. He was killed in the war!"

At the time, I did not appreciate his short words of advice: **"IT DOESN'T MATTER…!"**

He continued: "During your youth, your excuse may garner some extra attention or understanding of your failures. In the long run, however, it doesn't matter whether you have a father, a mother, a family, or any of the usual advantages given to most others who are more lucky than you. Life will treat you the way you treat life; the way you perform on your own initiative. You will need to compete with millions of other people for the fruits of life. Competitors just don't care that you may have started life at a disadvantage. You have no physical or mental disabilities holding you back. Others just won't carry you. Being successful and having a satisfactory life depends only on you. Others don't care that you were raised without your father. Your father's death cannot be your "crutch! **It just doesn't matter!**"

Like much of the advice I received from others along the way, I did not immediately put into action the kindly priest's strong words.

1957 Gus Gus G was the first contemporary two-wheel enthusiast I met through Ronnie, and we became lifelong friends thereafter.

Gus had moments of almost uncontrollable anger. The first time I experienced it, Ronnie and I were visiting Gus in his home workshop while he was working on his Triumph Terrier. Gus had converted this 150 cc motorcycle to an off-road racer, but he couldn't get the engine started on this particular day. Expressing his great frustration, Gus wailed away while beating the Terrier's gas tank with a hammer, and then threw the Terrier down the hill behind his shop.

This was a good learning experience for me, as I then knew to avoid him when he was growing exceedingly frustrated.

1957 ff Enduro Sundays On many Sundays, we would participate in on/off-road competitions, with the prize being prestige and a trophy. These "enduros" were timed events, with directional signs posted along the way to guide riders to their destination. Arrival times at surprise check points determined the number of points awarded to each rider. Some competitors rode singly, while others rode dual. As portions of the route often included hazards of deep sand or mud, having a dual rider who could help push the motorcycle through the hazard was an advantage.

On this particular Sunday afternoon, I was unable to find a rider who needed a dual rider, so I stayed home. Gus drove his Velocette (Velo), and Ronnie rode dual behind him. Attempting to make up lost time, Gus speeded and lost control on a country gravel road, crashing into a tree. Gus was critically injured and remained on life support for several days, while Ronnie was treated for cuts and bruises, and released.

Such was the type of risk that came with being an enthusiast, providing parents yet another source of great worry.

Gus recovered. Ronnie recovered.

1957 Summer Jobs Don often found summer employment for us.

Job #8 was with a house mover. Crawling under enormous houses being lifted by hydraulic jacks so the house could be moved just a few inches at a time paid well.

Preparing for work the first day, while riding my stepfather's new 600 cc Norton motorcycle (without his knowledge), I went shopping for quality work gloves, but I failed to apply the brakes when all traffic in front of me stopped. The resulting impact sent me and the brand new motorcycle flying through the air. Fortunately, I landed running, and the motorcycle landed right-side up on its center stand, facing the other direction. Although the motorcycle was damaged, I was able to ride it away from the accident and park it behind our house. I then hurried to start my house mover job, without gloves and with no reasonable explanation in mind for my step-father's mangled motorcycle.

But, doggone it, the experience showed that moving houses is hard and dangerous work. Three days was enough for me.

Job #9, also with Don, was at a pickle factory fifteen miles from our houses. Farmers would bring in their cucumber harvests. We would sort the "cucs" according to size, weigh them, and put them in the appropriate vat of brine for transformation into pickles. These vats were wooden and huge, standing about 15 feet high and at least 15 feet in diameter. A strong board, stretched across the top of each vat, allowed for walking to the center of the vat to facilitate dropping ingredients into the brine. The brine formula was the following: a layer of water followed by a layer of cucumbers followed by a layer of salt, repeated several times until the vat was full.

There were at least 30 vats of similar size at the pickle plant. Commuting together on stepfather's damaged Norton motorcycle at ridiculously high and reckless speeds, we worked both day and night shifts, depending on the workload and when the farmers could deliver their cucumbers.

Being relatively new to the pickling labor force, and not particularly liking the alcohol-infused owner/manager of the pickle factory, and further not liking the impact of night working hours on our night social lives, we did not appreciate being assigned to the night shift.

To express our dissatisfaction with "the Man", we would often add our own special "ingredients" to the brine. This happened only at night when the boss could not see us improving on his recipe.

Suffice it to say, it was years before we ate pickles again!

1957 Job #10 Pick 1, pick 2, pick 3…pick 8, arrange nicely, staple, stack, and start again — 200 times each month.

Such was the routine in assembling the monthly newsletter at Lynn's Motorcycle Shop. It wasn't the 75-cent per hour generous wages that attracted me to Lynn's; rather, it was the opportunity to be around the people and machines that I enjoyed, while also gaining experience in the working world.

I usually hitched to Lynn's daily after school. After the usual 1-2 hours of work, getting home required another hitch.

A much wiser decision (**Life Lesson**, kids, pay attention) would have been to go home and do homework, of course, but for this 16 year-old, mine was definitely a youth-inspired choice. Those bright, shiny two-wheeled machines and the characters — young and old, rich and poor, bright and slow — who hung around the shop provided a great deal of real world knowledge that was impossible to find in books.

Lynn's owner was a physically slightly built, middle-aged man whose life experiences had produced an accomplished businessman. His past physical injuries precluded frequent riding, and he rarely climbed aboard a bike. I hanged around his business so often, he finally offered me a job. He seemed to like me and was a very understanding boss. If I couldn't make it to work for any reason, he did not become upset.

During the summers, he also had me do yard work at his very nice, corner lot, ranch style house. At those times, his wife, Phyllis, would usually invite me in for food and drink, Winston cigarettes, a game of cards, and some coming-of-age conversation. Phyllis was physically larger than Lynn. Both seemed comfortable in their marriage, which included no children. Lynn did not seem to notice that my hours spent away from his shop doing yard work at his house were excessively long, or, perhaps, he considered it a blessing.

In time, I was "promoted" to "mechanic's gopher". I ran errands, washed greasy motorcycles and parts, inventoried parts, cut chains, made bank runs, etc. The primary, and often only, mechanic was Kenny, a tall, lanky early 30's fellow. Kenny was distinguished by two main characteristics — his genius for fixing any mechanical problem/challenge and his obviously "patched-crotch" work pants.

My mechanical skills were greatly enhanced by Kenny's teaching. Also, when I worked full-time during the summer, he would give me a ride home for lunch and pick me up on his way back to work. These dual rides on his motorcycles were always exciting, and harrowing, as he made the lunch round trip in ever improving record times.

1957 ff Deadly Swelling On the negative side, I encountered a serious health issue while working at Lynn's.

A red, itchy rash suddenly appeared on my face and chest. While uncomfortable, I ignored it until I realized the saliva in my mouth was warming rapidly, and there was a swelling in my throat and windpipe. Sensing a potentially serious threat to my well-being, the boss suggested I go home. Kenny gave me a speedy ride home, where my mother immediately decided I needed to receive emergency treatment.

By the time we arrived at the ER, the hives had overtaken my entire body. Individual mini-hives had combined with others until my entire outer skin appeared as one gigantic hive, stretching from nose to toes and entering the many orifices in between, and breathing had become nearly impossible!

The itching was most uncomfortable, but the difficult breathing was most dangerous. The ER folks knew what to do, injecting me immediately with adrenalin. The hives retreated en masse, and my hope for an earthly future returned.

Benadryl pills were my constant companion for years thereafter.

1957 ff Bean Bowl I discovered the Bean Bowl while searching for a new place to enjoy evening eats.

The Bean Bowl seated only ten — all at the counter. Beyond the counter labored a cook and the waitress/manager. The four feet between the counter's stools and the back wall provided space for us guys to congregate. Most of us were in our middle to late teens. Most of those still enrolled in high school were attending trade classes — metal working, auto repairs, carpentry, painting, etc. This was a time when technical/blue collar career skills could be learned in high school without the distraction of hours of required English, History, Math, etc., homework. Life was good!

There was no required entrance exam to become a member of the Bean Bowl group. Mostly, you just showed up and didn't disrupt the ambiance. Some members had nicknames. The most memorable member's nickname was "Bones," attached to a very skinny kid with a better-than-new shiny black, 1951 Ford coupe with a V8 engine and dual exhausts.

A cheeseburger with a bowl of chili was the most popular delicacy at the Bean Bowl.

Arrival time week-nights was usually about 6:30 - 7:00 PM. After enjoying the usual delicacy, summer nights would find us standing outside on the corner, smoking (our own or others'), spitting, and generally acting like we owned the corner (to be clear, we did respect any elders passing by). Cars and motorcycles were the primary topics of discussion on the corner.

Saturdays were date nights for some, so Saturday action was sparse until 11:00 PM or later. Guys with steady girlfriends would not arrive until 1:00 - 2:00 AM or so, after they had finished their coeducational sports. Often, a contingent of the foolish would then play poker until the wee hours of the morning. It took me several years and many quarters to realize I had no future as an accomplished poker player. (**Life Lesson**, kids).

The Bowl was located on 6th Avenue, several miles north of downtown. I would usually arrive riding a motorcycle or driving Mom's car. Each evening's activities would inevitably include a ride in someone's car (the one that had enough gas) to downtown, around the downtown loop, and back up 6th Avenue to the Bowl. Seeing cool cars, especially those occupied by cool girls, was the main downtown attraction.

On rare occasion, fisticuffs with guys from other parts of town would occur. Fortunately, I was never involved in any fights as, like most of the Bean Bowl guys, I was a better runner than a fighter. Fists were the usual choice of weapon, although a sawed-off pool cue was becoming a quite popular companion. I kept one under the driver's seat of my car, but I never brandished it. Had the police ever stopped me and found the pool cue, my life would have certainly taken a different turn.

Typically, the only fights we won, we also lost, as the fights were often with other Bean Bowlers. One chronic loser, "Lucky," would, without even trying, somehow irritate another Bean Bowler almost nightly. Lucky held the unofficial record for the most lost fights on the corner, and he never seemed to learn why.

When the Bean Bowl wasn't full, the waitress/manager would let us play shuffleboard (without having purchased a delicacy) on the machine at the end of that four-foot wide passageway behind the counter's stools. She was a nice lady and Bean Bowlers would do anything for her. Though she would suffer us most of the time, there were occasions when she just couldn't take our antics anymore, and she would chase us out.

Levis were cool, as was a pack of Lucky Strike cigarettes rolled up in the sleeve of a white t-shirt. Ducktails, flattops, penny loafers, and toothpicks were in. Girlfriends shared their guy's driver's side of the front seat (how did the guy steer?), although few of the guys had girlfriends — at least, none whom they would bring to the Bowl where they would be taunted mercilessly by their "girlfriend-less" peers. Life was cool!

When the Bowl was full, or when we had been chased out by the waitress/manager, another favorite hangout was Chuck's Restaurant, half-way down the block and across the alley. For 75 cents, my favorite meal was spaghetti with one meatball, marinara sauce, and two slices of Italian bread with butter. Many nights, spaghetti with meatball beat cheeseburger with chili. Chuck's was also famous for pizza and onion rings. Chuck wouldn't let us hangout, though — we always had to order. And we had to leave as soon as our meal was finished.

1957 ff Bean Bowl Fun One warm summer night, I was transporting some friends around the loop in my family's '55 Studebaker (a really cool black and white two-door coupe). We came upon another Bean Bowl acquaintance driving his '57 Chevy, also filled with friends, around the loop. After rounding Capitol Hill and heading west down Grand Avenue, the drag race began.

Three police cars, sirens wailing and emergency lights flashing, appeared out of nowhere! We were informed by the boys in blue that we were exceeding 70 miles per hour before they stopped us (the Studebaker was winning, of course). We were then gifted with reckless driving tickets, resulting in a stern lecture from the judge and a $50 fine in traffic court and a much greater increase in auto insurance costs for my family.

On another summer evening, when returning north on 6th Avenue, the police stopped me. I was driving my stepfather's 1950 Mercury sedan, which had months earlier suffered a ripped left rear fender which had not yet been repaired. That piece of the fender hanging precipitously out from the car and bouncing with each bump in the road may have been what invited the curiosity of the boys in blue. Or, maybe it was the tailpipe bouncing off the street at each bump. In any event, they stopped me and searched the car thoroughly, pulling out seats and carpets, looking for a reason to "take me downtown." With nothing illegal being found (the pool cue had stayed home that night), they suggested I might want to retire for the evening and stay out of trouble. Had they searched me and found the illegal fireworks in the high-top engineer boots I was wearing, my life would likely have taken a radical turn.

As referenced previously, drag racing was often a part of the evening activity for Bean Bowlers. Whether it was a parent's car (as was mostly the case with me) or a guy's own hot rod, we had to test one against the other. Gus and I tested our mothers' cars on several occasions - his mom's 1955 Mercury 2-door hardtop versus my Mom's really cool, black and white, two-door 1955 Studebaker coupe. On short runs, on city streets, the Mercury would always win. On longer runs, on the new freeway around the north side of the city, the Studebaker would win, always coming on strong at the end of the run. Gus, a mechanical wiz, was always amazed at the cam the Studebaker must have had. I don't know what it was, but winning was fun — even in your mother's exceptionally cool car!

Bean Bowlers had our own form of "Code Blue!" When someone yelled "Code Blue!", everyone scattered, for it meant the police were about to pounce. For some (many) reason(s), the city police (some of whom were probably Bean Bowl graduates) did not want us congregating on the corner. The elder senior citizens who had to navigate through our smoke and spittle to reach their destinations undoubtedly lodged complaints. With threat of incarceration, the police would order us to disband (apparently loitering was illegal), which we would do until they were out of sight. Of course, they would return, sometime sneaking up the alley with car lights off, causing us to initiate "Code Blue!" again.

(Please note — Although a "gang" congregating on a street corner might have seemed threatening to some, I want to again emphasize our "gang" would have come to the aid of any senior citizen who might have been actually threatened.)

The Bowl was a great place to learn about life — from our peers — who likely knew less about life than they boasted.

Sadly, the Bean Bowl exists no longer. A dull, drab, non-essential, insurance agency office replaced it.

I wonder how the kids of today will learn about life's essential secrets — without a Bean Bowl.

(ORP man understands)

("ORP man", the voice of the ordinary, rational, and prudent person buried deep within our being, provides so-often-ignored counsel for some of our decisions, and then reflects on those decisions).

1958 Job #11 Before an opening was available at Lynn's this year, Stepfather Jim arranged a job for me at the plant where he worked as a welder.

I sand blasted concrete forms eight hours daily, outside in the miserably hot summer sun, while peering through the glass window in the canvas hood, with misty oxygen fed into the hood for breathing. This watery mist then dripped down through the hood and onto my clothes, drenching my clothes and pulling sand into every crook and crevice of my body. Pay was ok, but it was hard, nasty work.

Two weeks of this, and I joyfully moved on and returned to Lynn's.

1958 Racing While working at Lynn's, I became interested in racing. I had saved enough to purchase a Triumph Tiger Cub, which had been previously raced by its owner. Big Mistake! It was in the shop more often than on the race track. I eventually sold it to a friend and co-worker of stepfather Jim. The friend soon learned the same lesson I had learned previously — never purchase a used motorcycle that had been a racer. (Perhaps the friend also learned another lesson — be cautious when buying used, mechanical things from a friend.)

With the proceeds, I purchased an older, worn and torn Triumph 500cc motorcycle and began racing it. While mechanical failures prevented me from ever finishing a race, the burning light had been lit for racing.

(ORP man was concerned)

1958 ff Carol As I was proceeding slowly through my teen years, Carol was careening through hers.

Carol loved many. Romance seemed always just around the corner. Then she met David, a very good-looking 18 year-old. He, too, took Carol on long car trips around and outside of town. He drove a black, 1941 Ford 2-door sedan — and drove quite irresponsibly, I must say, which I know because this little tag-along brother experienced a most harrowing ride one evening that included rounding corners exceedingly fast, balanced on only two wheels.

As it turned out, driving wasn't the only thing he was doing irresponsibly, and Carol became pregnant. A quick trip to the Justice of the Peace (the same JP previously visited by Mom and Jim) ensued. A cake and refreshments followed in our little house at 205 H, and then they were off to a new life together forever.

In due time, a handsome son, Kelly, was born. David took several jobs to support them, but in less than two years, the marriage ended.

Summer 1958 First Love Two things happened this summer that set the tone for my future. Friend Ronnie decided enlisting in the Navy would be best for his future, and Don persuaded me to join him at a teen dance. Since I was never comfortable with my dancing skills, I was reluctant to go, but Ronnie's leaving town opened many hours for other activities, so I went dancing and am forever thankful that he began serving his country when he did.

Almost immediately upon entering the dance club, Don introduced me to a pretty, five-foot-two, beautiful brunette, attired in a white sailor hat, white and blue blouse resembling a sailor's uniform, white shorts, and white tennies. Her smile and enthusiasm captured me immediately, as she faced me, standing on my toes. I learned much later that our meeting had been pre-arranged by Don and his new girlfriend, so that we would all have dating partners for our senior year activities. Sally and I began our personal relationship as a logistical arrangement.

"Rockin' Robin" played for our first dance, through which I blundered awkwardly. She promised I would improve with her tutelage and frequent repetition. The evening went well and ended with a promise for a date soon. When I arrived home, somehow her perfumed hankie mysteriously appeared in my pocket (it rested on my pillow for days/weeks/months thereafter). Our first date could not come soon enough!

With that beginning, Sally and I had embarked on our "first love" relationship — a love that lasts forever, is never forgotten, and the memory of which gets sweeter over time.

I was nervous when I arrived at her house for our first date. Her father was reclining on the living room couch, watching the Friday night fights on TV, and he neglected to even acknowledge my presence when Sally attempted to introduce me. I suspect, as a father of four girls (two older), he had little appreciation for the "natural" attraction boys had toward his daughters. I felt "persona non grata"! (Months later, as would be expected, he fell to my charms.)

Our senior year was marked by many great parties and by the typical break-ups and make-ups of young lovers, but Sally and I believed we were destined to be together — eventually. Sally's "eventually" included us being married at Christmas time, three and one-half years hence, following her graduation from nurses training, in St. John's church, with the wedding party decorated in joyous reds and whites, just like her two older sisters had done. I did not dispute her plan.

(ORP man chuckled.)

Christmas 1958 Oops! When picking up Sally at church, I tapped the brakes too late and slid on the icy parking lot into the church wall, damaging Mom's new, Chinese red, '58 Studebaker Silver Hawk. The church pastor believed it was not the fault of the icy parking lot. Of course I disagreed. Everyone knows, for the safety of the parishioners, church parking lots should always be salted and ice-free!

1959 Me and Church My relationship with church remained fairly stable through the high school years — transgression, guilt, forgiveness; transgression, guilt, forgiveness - repeated endlessly.

My all-male Catholic high school required its students to make an annual retreat, providing the opportunity for prayerful insight and a required confession. Confession was conducted face-to-face with a designated priest. Confession being an uncomfortable situation for male adolescents anyway, adding the face-to-face element created additional discomfort.

In the middle of my confession, which included some "sins" with an un-named girlfriend, the priest offered her name and commented: "She must be a really attractive girl!"

I left confused!

Years later, this priest was defrocked. Appropriate!

May 1959 Graduation High school graduation finally came, and 205 H was cleaned and ready for all the relatives and other guests to help celebrate my achievement. My expectations were high, both to see long-missed relatives, and, perhaps, to reap the benefit of their monetary gifts. Invitations with photos had been sent timely to the same relatives who had helped cousin Yvonne celebrate two years previously. Mom, Jim, Carol, Sally and I were groomed and ready.

Disappointment! None of the invitees arrived to help us celebrate.

In spite of that, Sally and I had a very good night!

(ORP man became concerned.)

Summer 1959 Big Moment A big moment in a young man's life! - I got my first, "owned" car — a faded, blue and rusty, six-cylinder, worn and torn, 1951 Ford 2-door sedan. For $175, what could be better! Thanks, Mom!

Calling it a "project" car would be an understatement, but paint the wheel rims Chinese red, install fake whitewalls, install a rear-seat speaker, hang a rosary on the rear-view mirror, then speed away! It was a day of unequalled joy!

1959 Bean Bowl Tragedies An incident occurred when Lucky, Gus, and I were on a road trip to Peoria's motorcycle races in my '51. While I was driving, Lucky irritated Gus to the point that Gus (who was twice Lucky's size) angrily began beating him. Gus was both sorry and apologetic afterwards, but Lucky just never learned how to not irritate others, and he suffered more beatings from "friends" over the Bean Bowl years.

On another summer night, I agreed to give Lucky a ride home on the motorcycle I was driving (the very same, not-so-cool, Norton, belonging to stepfather Jim, that I had crashed previously). As was customary, when leaving the Bean Bowl parking lot, Bowlers would burn rubber or otherwise demonstrate how loud and fast was their vehicle. With Lucky riding behind and the megaphone exhausts screaming, we flew out of the Bowl's parking lot, making a slight lean to the left to proceed down the street at speed. The next thing I recalled, Lucky and I were both lying on the pavement in agony, bloody and hurting. (**Life Lesson, kids** — Always retract the kickstand on the motorcycle before engaging the gears. When moving and leaning slightly, an extended kickstand will dig into the pavement, causing the motorcycle, riders and all to travel in an unintended direction).

Fortunately, we did not require hospitalization (we were tough, if not very smart).

Tragically, Lucky was killed months later in an automobile accident.

Another Bean Bowl tragedy occurred when "Jim" (not stepfather James Eugene) and Gus were motorcycle racing in a sanctioned event in Oskaloosa, Iowa. It was a dirt, short-track race, and Jim fell down in a corner. Unfortunately, Gus was right behind and, unable to avoid Jim, struck his head. Sadly, Jim's helmet did not prevent fatal injuries.

While Bowl time was usually fun, not everyone survived.

Summer 1959 Conflicting Loves The summer before college was eventful. Sally convinced me attending college would provide a better future life for us than would my continuing on as a motorcycle mechanic. Paying for college would have been impossible had it not been for the benefit provided by the US Government pursuant to my father's death while on active duty. So, I sent an application to the college Sally recommended (which her brother-in-law had attended) and was speedily accepted. The course was set.

I continued to race as often as possible. Races were always on Sunday, so most of my Sundays were spent at the racetrack rather than with Sally and our high school friends at the picnics, the pool, and other places she preferred. Sally accompanied me to a race one particular Sunday, where I crashed and incurred a few scrapes and bruises, further mystifying her as to why I enjoyed this activity. She finally gave me an ultimatum to spend more time, Sundays especially, with her.

While I enjoyed our time together, I resisted giving up my cherished racing. I continued racing on Sundays, and we managed through our first major relationship trauma — bruised but not broken.

At end of summer, I sold my racing machine and prepared for my next phase of life — college — "eventually" followed by marriage!

(ORP man smiled)

Aug 1959 Arriving at College College visits? What were those? Perhaps it was something the rich kids did, but I was not aware of such and had never made a college visit. In fact, during my early high school years, I never even thought about attending college. All I wanted to do was graduate from high school and get on with my life.

In one of those periodic teacher/student conferences I disdained so much, a Catholic priest, knowing of my interest in motorcycles and mechanics, suggested I go to a General Motors Mechanics Training Center to better prepare for life after high school as a skilled mechanic. It sounded good, but meeting Sally had changed all that, as she passionately encouraged me to attend college.

I had never been on a college campus. But, there I was, in August 1959, getting ready for college. After buying some new clothes (2 pairs of wash pants, a few shirts, and some underwear), I was ready to go. Appropriate good-byes were exchanged, separately with Sally and then with Mom and Carol, I placed my two suitcases into the Chinese red, 1958 Studebaker Silver Hawk, hopped in, and rode away, with Stepfather Jim driving and friend Gregory R riding along. I nearly wept when leaving my '51 at home.

The 130 mile drive to “Big Town” was uneventful, but upon nearing the college campus, we encountered a “mini tornado” propelling dirt and assorted trash through the air. Compounded by the stifling smells from the stockyards, I mentally questioned the wisdom of Sally’s roadmap.

In spite of that initial concern, we pushed on. After locating my assigned dormitory (an upper classmen’s dorm where late-applying freshmen were assigned), I grabbed my two suitcases, said goodbyes to Jim and Gregory at the curb, and entered the dormitory (by a door which I subsequently discovered was to be used only as an exit — the first of many freshman mistakes to come). Another phase in my life had begun…

I had become a collegian!!

No one had prepared me for what college would be like. After securing my dorm room, and not knowing what else to do, old habits took over, and I immediately headed to the closest motorcycle shop, proving again that too much change all at once is just too much!

(ORP man was confused)

Sep 1959 College Roommates Sharing a dorm room with a new acquaintance can be quite enlightening and educational in many different ways, which is a multi-edged sword. But at least the bed was an upgrade from my sofa at home!

My first freshman roommate was Dennis Y, a Hawaiian. Dennis did not want to be here, and he was intent on making his stay short. He was missing his HTH (home-town-honey) in Honolulu and was confident that never attending class was his best way to get a ticket home. He slept or partied instead. It worked, and Dennis did not return for the second semester.

Second semester roommate was Gary F, a recently expelled freshman from a Minnesota Catholic college. After one semester here, he was re-admitted in Minnesota. Unlike Dennis Y, he studied continually.

I have heard from neither of them since.

Sep 1959 ff Sleepers’ Mass Late night studies made early arising quite challenging.

All full-time students were required to attend Mass each Thursday at 9:00 AM, where attendance was monitored by each student signing and submitting an attendance card during the mass (Thursday mass attendance was, of course, in addition to the church-required Sunday mass attendance, where the only monitor was one’s personal Catholic guilt).

If needed, some fraternity brothers who distributed and collected the Thursday attendance cards might even validate the attendance cards for those of us who preferred to sleep in.

Perhaps that is why we “sleepers” missed timely hearing of the changes from the mid-sixties’ Vatican II — the convocation of bishops that made many changes in church liturgy and other dictates.

Thursday mass was both a religious and a social event. The priests used it to pass on spiritual & moral admonitions. Many students used it especially as a gathering place, followed with social time in the student center.

(GPA 3.0 fall 1959; 2.53 spring 1960)

Summer 1960 College Year One During my freshman year in college, I realized our precious "first love" had begun to be something of a burden for me. The academic courses were challenging, and new experiences, new female attractions, and the 130 mile separation all combined to weaken my commitment to Sally. Especially damaging was Sally's discovery that I had covertly "kept company" with her best friend, Kay C., who was then attending a college near me (Hey! A guy gets lonely!). Kay's loyalty to friendship exceeded her attraction to me, and she spilled the beans!

A very difficult discussion with Sally followed. We reconciled and our relationship resumed, fully committed to her "eventually" roadmap.

Somewhat related to that commitment, my first day home after successfully completing freshman year was spent on an all-nighter, researching, composing, and typing a term paper Sally had due the very next morning. I still wonder if her teacher, a priest who knew us well (he was the coolest priest/teacher I had had in high school) suspected who actually prepared the paper when he saw us visiting briefly in the nursing school parking lot at 7:30 AM that morning, as I passed the completed term paper to Sally. (Of no real significance to this memoir, the priest later left the Catholic Church and became an Episcopalian priest so he could marry.)

Summer 1960 Wow! Summer vacation excitement continued that week when I received an overwhelming surprise — stepfather Jim presented me with a brand new, 1961 Triumph 500 cc racing motorcycle, which was then, in my circle of friends, the latest and greatest motorcycle available for racing!

Sally was not enthused!

Summer 1960 Surprise The many work experiences I gained at his shop, and the familial affection gained at his house, ensured me I had a grand future at Lynn's, so I assumed a job would be waiting there for me that summer — until real life slapped me right in the face the day I arrived at the shop and was introduced to Lynn's nephew, who was most skillfully pulling pages (Pick 1, pick 2, pick 3…pick 8), washing parts, and smoking Winstons.

Other, less satisfying and less memorable, summer jobs were found.

Life Lesson, Kids: Assumption often leads to disappointment!

Summer 1960 Mom's Rule One particularly memorable Sunday that summer occurred at a race track. During a heat race, two racers crashed ahead of me, and I hit them, spilling myself and my bike onto the dirt track. As is protocol in such situations, the race was halted, and the crashed racers were given the opportunity to fix their bruised equipment, arms and legs, and restart behind the rest of the racers.

Against my better judgment, Mom had come with us that Sunday. She had remained in our sunbaked, parked car until the crash occurred, but the crash brought her out to the starting line, where she stood in front of me and the other racers (most of whom knew me as a determined, gritty, tough racer), proclaiming that she was my mother, I was still a minor, and I was finished racing for the day — one of the most embarrassing moments in my young life! (Kind of hilarious, in retrospect!)

My racing continued during the summer (sans Mom), which was still filled with many good times for Sally and me, but as I left for the start of my sophomore year, we agreed to remain close, but not exclusive, as a test of our relationship.

(ORP man was skeptical.)

Summer 1960 ff Deadly Swelling Still Over the years, the hives had returned periodically, with varying degrees of severity. Whenever saliva in my mouth began to warm, I knew another hectic trip to the ER was needed, as an adrenalin shot would always provide relief.

Between ER visits, Benadryl pills, which offered limited relief, were ingested when symptoms appeared. The pills were prescribed by Dr. Noun after my first bout with the hives. But after several visits, Dr. Noun, who I years later realized was quite wise, had suggested a different kind of medicine to cure my ills.

"Don't worry so much! Things will be ok!" was his advice.

He apparently surmised that the death of my father and the resulting issues my family had and were still facing, and the usual experiences of maturing (puberty, challenges in school, learning about women, living poorly, global threats of nuclear war and destruction, etc., etc.), all had some role to play in the cause of my hives.

So, following his advice, I soon adopted Mad Magazine's Alfred E. Neuman's, "What, Me Worry?" approach to life! I learned that an initial "chuckle", accompanied with a smile, at the moment of most "tragedies", is calming, and provides time to develop clearer thinking about any corrective action needed.

Most mountains then became molehills! Hives became less frequent.

I remain most grateful to Mad Magazine, Alfred E. Neuman, and Dr. Noun for teaching me how to chill.

Summer 1960 Sad Ending Brother-in-law David decided, for whatever reason, to end their marriage, and Carol was left to raise Kelly on her own. David soon moved to California and never provided for them again.

Nonetheless, Carol worked hard and managed to provide for her son — often with a little help from those who loved them — her family.

Sep 1960 Me and Dave Returning to college for my sophomore year of "studies" (at that point, I was still determined to earn very good grades), Dave R was descending the front steps of the men's dormitory as I was arriving. A glee clubber in high school, he was singing a tune as we met. As I would soon discover, Dave was always singing some tune.

Although I barely remembered Dave from our freshman year, we mysteriously, immediately bonded and became good friends and constant companions. We pledged the same fraternity; we both took part-time retail sales jobs at downtown stores (**Job #12**, mine included polishing and selling shoes at a department store, quickly curing me of retailing!); we double-dated and partied together.

Being among the many poor students in college, both Dave and I often had to choose between essentials and luxuries. Still, Dave had difficulty saving his very limited funds for just those essentials, so one day he handed me all his cash, asking that I not give it back to him except for the purchase of essentials. I managed his treasury accordingly, but after I allowed his $14 treasury to become depleted with only the purchase of essentials, he never asked me to be his personal treasurer again.

Sep 1960 Second Time Around Having been confirmed at the age of 12 with a slap on the cheek from the bishop, I took seriously my required vow to abstain from alcoholic beverages until the age of 21. Keeping that vow was difficult for me because I had previously learned to enjoy the ½ bottle of beer allotted to me daily by my Great Uncle Ben when working the farm fields in prior summers. He would, thankfully, scratch the beer bottle label at the "½ empty/full point", allowing me to drink to the scratch but no more. I hated giving that up.

But desiring to not become an alcoholic, loser-man like some who had wandered through our family's lives, it was a good vow for me to take.

And I faithfully observed that vow until one night at the beginning of my sophomore year, when I accompanied Dave R and Don D (not the Don S mentioned previously, who was a lifelong friend) to a small party where, heaven forbid, students were drinking beer! Well, (while mentally apologizing to the bishop), I had made it to age 20, so I deemed that to be sufficient to satisfy my vow. Two beers later, I was unable to even stand unassisted, let alone walk back to my dorm room. Getting there would require passing the open door of the dorm monitor's office. Understand, the monitor was a priest who enthusiastically enjoyed catching any student who broke any of the rules — especially the one prohibiting imbibing in alcoholic beverages.

So, what does this have to do with the "Second Time Around"?

I had recently become enthralled with a beautiful, black-haired freshman named Bernie (Bernadette). However, I was not yet ready to tell the world, nor Bernie, of my feelings. But with a tongue loosened by those 2 beers, and with slurred words, I expressed my secret feelings to Dave and Don, who then felt compelled to drive to Bernie's dorm and introduce an inebriated me to this lovely lady — in front of several of her roommates — before walking me to my dorm.

Dave and Don quietly, quickly, and foolishly walked me past the dorm monitor's door and deposited me, safely, in my bed, before curfew. Had we been caught by the monitor, our college careers would have been vastly changed! Thanks, guys!

The following day, I recovered and expressed my sincere apologies to Bernie for the embarrassment the three of us had caused, but it was the ice-breaker that provided the start of our several year relationship. An attractive and intelligent young woman, she, of course, became equally enthralled with me. And since my relationship with Sally was cooling, and since a Sinatra song titled "Second Time Around" was currently popular, our theme became "Second Time Around." Cute, huh!

Bernie was from a Navy family. Her father had achieved a high, non-commissioned officer rank and had retired the family to his small, nearby rural hometown. Bernie was pursuing a nursing career, and the military was paying her college expenses in return for her commitment to serve.

Our relationship grew stronger, with visits to each's homes and families. 2nd times were good!

(ORP man was optimistic)

Fall 1960 Inspiration from Home During a particularly difficult and challenging time in the first semester of my sophomore year, I was considering leaving college for a number of reasons, including girl issues, concern for family, and shortage of funds. Somehow Mom got a sense of my "troubles" and sent the following letter—

Dear Michael,

I hope you are keeping up on the speeches made at the United Nations. Never before in history have there been so many important things unfolding every day in the news. Too bad we don't have a strong leader and one who was loved like Franklin Roosevelt. He fit so naturally in the White House. It was just like home for him — because that's where he belonged. He leisurely had breakfast in bed — looked over his mail in bed — even Fala thought it was his home. He didn't have to knock himself out knocking a golf-ball around the nearest golf-course wherever he was.

The more necessary it becomes for great planning and leadership for our government, the only decision Ike can make is to go out for a game of golf!

My idea is that you can't spend all leisure time and accomplish much deep thinking by using up the last of your energy at the Bean Bowl and the motorcycle shops. God gave you the brains to use and you sure can't rush into some doctor's office — half listen — rush out, not even ask the most important questions — expect someone else to have the answers or later on to have someone else ask the questions and get the answers.

Considerable time and thought should be taken for important things and then if there is any excess time left over, you might see what the boys are doing, but I'm sure they will be doing and saying the same things five years from now, unless they have a different P.O. address.

Remember all you must do now is discipline yourself and prepare that you will be "Master of Your House" — and never expect the burden to be carried by anyone else. You never know when you will be called upon in life to help, and how heartbreaking it will be if you can only stand by and think, "Maybe if I had done so and so, I could have helped."

So let no one or no thing interfere or divert your chance to get an education. Remember the devil works even through Christians to reach his target. Make a good retreat and pray that your back will not give you too much trouble this year. We all love you, hope you feel the same about us. Try to enjoy your hard assignments — you know, give yourself an old "pep talk". Soon you will believe it.

Stop into chapel or church for a short time and notice the beauty in the architecture and the coloring and say a short prayer — or don't even say a prayer. Or just say, "I'm here, I don't feel so good — don't let anything get me down". Then kick the pew and leave. "I'll be back when I feel better."

I don't know everything, but I don't think you need to take it out on Sally. Of course, you may not know just what you are going to be doing in the next few years, but you know that we are with you — going to work, not wallowing in drunkenness, etc., and we are satisfied and happy and trying to be able to help you by keeping our senses — so you won't have to worry at the present about us. Just one thing in life doesn't bring happiness. And your college studies will result in a wider scope of interests — an interest in people — good reading, etc.

Love
Your Mom

Thanks, Mom!

Fall 1960 Expanding Scope My "scope" of interests were, indeed, expanding, and my concept of "eventually" became sometime much further out in the future — an undefined time after I had experienced much more of the "scope". But I still had Sally in my heart and, hopefully, in my future, though I mentally resisted being somewhat pressured towards that future.

Nov 1960 I Got the Bug Fatigued by the accumulated impact of social, academic, and work activities, the virus hit! The campus doc admitted me immediately.

While I was hospitalized for infectious mononucleosis, Bernie led a group of my fraternity brothers for a surreptitious visit after hours, bringing with them, of course, the traditional beverages of any fraternity party. The nursing staff and the attending doc were not pleased!

Upon release, all social activities resumed.

(GPA 2.60 fall 1960)

Mar 1961 College Roommates 2.0 This year's roommate was Jim G, an interesting, fun kid from Iowa. We spent one weekend constructing his mail order "easy-to-build, all 1000+parts included", stereo system kit, only to learn, upon completion, we should have soldered each part as it was added rather than waiting until all parts had been affixed. His future as an electrical engineer became questionable.

Jim was quite annoying at night, as he often made disturbing noises under his sheets while sleeping.

But a big plus was that he had a car. On a beautiful, afternoon spring day, he took three of us on a ride with the top down. First, pickup beer. Second, squeal tires around busy downtown intersection. Third, interact verbally with a local policeman who questioned why we were being so foolish. Fourth, dump the beer and hurry back to the dorm before the policeman reconsidered and assessed a more serious punishment.

Close call!

Apr 1961 Student Council Elections Our fraternity nominated Dave and me to run for Student Board of Governors, a highly prestigious position and resume' enhancer.

Dave could sometimes become somewhat intense. Things tended to excite and bother him. For instance, when an observer pointed out Dave had misspelled "Knowledgeable" (a qualifying characteristic) as "Knowledgable" on the huge campaign poster he had displayed in the Student Center to promote his election, he became seriously distraught. I, on the other hand, thought it was ingenious marketing, as the missing letter gained widespread attention from the voters. It was hilarious!!

Neither Dave nor I was elected to the Board, though we did survive the primary. In hindsight, it was for the best, as serving in the position would have conflicted with our many other very serious social and work activities.

Apr 1961 Fire Emergency Driving the '51 on the way back to school after Easter break, my planned stop to pick up Bernie at her parent's home turned into a minor emergency — the rear floor carpet was smoldering and on fire. The exhaust heat from a hole in the top of the rusted muffler was the cause. Removing the carpet solved the fire problem, but you wouldn't want to sit in that rear seat with your feet on the floor thereafter.

Why her parents would then allow her to ride with me in that car will always be a mystery, but Bernie and I did arrive safely back on campus.

Jun 1961 Oops! While home on summer vacation, an evening errand turned into a nightmare when an oncoming car turned left in front of me, and we collided. How that accident turned out to be my fault, I still do not comprehend, but my auto insurance cost increased again.

The resulting mysterious noise from the engine caused me to retire the '51 and replace it with an equally poorly cared for '49 V8 Ford sedan — a steal at $125.00, even though it tilted downward at the left front, the trunk lid flew open with each bump encountered, the headlights went mysteriously out at the most inopportune times, and it had more than its fair share of body rust.

I transferred the "good" parts, including those majestic Chinese red wheels and the rear-seat speaker, from the '51 to the '49, parked the '51 behind Mom's garage where the pigeon coop had once been located, and off I sped.

The '49 was now my daily ride.

(To my knowledge, the '51 sits behind that garage still today.)

Jun 1961 Missteps College was a great academic success my freshman year, having attained a 3.00 and a 2.53 grade point average the first two semesters, respectively. Like so many other students, however, initial great success was followed by a succession of poorer and poorer academic achievements.

It wasn't that I lost interest — I simply gained competing interests. My goals changed from achieving outstanding academic success to simply graduating with a respectable degree and obtaining employment which would allow me to live above ground, out of the typical young graduate's basement room rental with the high humidity and various types of creepy crawlers; to be able to acquire an automobile that could be driven more miles than it had to be pushed; to generally start what I deemed would be a very successful life; and to assist my family financially. However, there was one major obstacle that arose — Thomistic philosophy.

The university required all students to take a certain number of theology classes and a certain number of Thomistic philosophy courses. "Philosophy of Being" was followed by "Philosophy of Man" and at least two other related courses. I have to tell you — this stuff did not make sense. "Essence" and "Existence" are two concepts I recall from those classes. I didn't understand them then, and I still don't!

But from those courses I did learn one great lesson — never write a note to the professor, a priest in this case, on the blue book final exam, your true feelings about the course. To quote my only writing on the final exam in the "Philosophy of Man" course (the first time I took the class): "I don't understand a thing you have said all semester!"

(ORP man floundered!)

(GPA 2.13 Spring 1961 when Philosophy of Man's "F" is included/2.67 when excluded)

Sep 1961 Extra-Curricular Education 101 Fraternity parties were often held in a remodeled barn about 10 miles south of the university. After one of those parties, having entirely too many bourbon and sevens, the late night drive back at the end of the party was particularly hazardous as we, with me driving my tilting, rusty 1949 Ford V8 sedan carrying Dave and our dates, and with eyes unable to clearly discern multiple images of objects even when the headlights worked properly, traveled the distance, including through the challenging south business district, and arrived back on campus safely. Thank God! Henry, my guardian angel, must have been looking after us!

Sep 1961 College Off Campus The university's strict rules did not allow students to live off-campus, unless it was in approved housing. Following rules, as I always do, I had moved into an approved boarding house. That lasted for 5 days. Our very nice landlady followed the university's rules and made sure we were in our rooms by 8:00 PM Sunday through Thursday, and10:30 PM on Friday and Saturday. Such a tortured existence!

Talk about timing! After successfully dodging the housing rules by other means, including the help of a married fraternity brother and his wife who owned their own house and vouched that we did, in fact, board with them, Dave and I found jobs (**Job #13**) with some real perks off-campus at the OEA Teachers' Manor, a retirement facility for elderly public school teachers (wonderful folks, actually). These jobs provided "university-approved" housing. (If they had only known…!)

In return for our totally exhaustive duties in the Teachers' kitchen during and after each evening meal, we were compensated with room and all-we-could-eat evening meals. Fortunately, Bernie was still living on-campus and had a cafeteria "all-you-can-eat" food plan, so her noon "seconds" became the primary source of my Monday through Friday noon nutrition.

Our OEA room was a second-floor apartment suitable for two people of very modest means, having very few possessions (that perfectly described Dave and me). Two beds, two closets, a bathroom, and two desks with chairs were provided. It was a perfect arrangement for two hard-working, hard-studying college students.

It was also a perfect place to have visitors of the female type, except that our lady boss, another strict disciplinarian, resided in an apartment at the other end of the same floor, and Teachers' arrangement with the university forbade allowing female visitors in our room at any time.

Although such rules created a challenge to our social development, when the occasion demanded, we would wait until late in the evening, when the boss lady should be sleeping, before sneaking the forbidden visitors through the underground garage, up the back stairway, and into our room — muffling laughter as we sprinted the final 50 feet to our door. (N.B. Lest there be any misunderstanding, Bernie was never fortunate to be a guest there.)

The process was reversed when "visiting hours" were over.

One might wonder if all this clandestine activity was worth the effort, since the penalty, had we been caught, of being suspended from college could be life altering. One might wonder…

(ORP man was disappointed!)

Nov 1961 Deep Thoughts Emerge Until I began studying philosophy in college, I had no concerns with any of the Catholic Church's teachings. I faithfully memorized and believed everything the stern nuns had taught us. There was never a question of their veracity. Sisters Paula, Loretta, Mary, Cecilia, Father Maher and others were to be believed — or else!

Simultaneously experiencing the radical Vatican II changes taking place in Church and learning from the required philosophy courses to "think", not just memorize, I began to contemplate the universal and unanswerable: "Why?"

Some of the changes were obvious.

All those beautiful altars, on which the priests, with their backs to the congregation, prepared the Eucharist, were being replaced by mostly unremarkable, Germanic-style tables, behind which the priests now faced the congregation when preparing the Eucharist.

Catholics could now eat red meat on Fridays, and we could now meet our Sunday mass obligation on Saturday evening instead of just on Sunday (those stern grade school nuns and Father Maher were turning in their respective graves on that one)!

But we would still have sin (mortal & venial), and we would still have confession.

Great mysteries still abound, the greatest of which is the Eucharist, as do the other great mysteries of Mary, the Blessed Mother, such as the virgin birth and the assumption with her human body intact.

Nagging questions began to emerge for me at this time, such as —

> Is Christ really God (i.e., the son of God)? Is there really a third-person God (i.e., the Holy Ghost/Spirit)?
>
> Does a priest really turn bread & wine into the real body & blood of Christ?
>
> Do kids who sin in their teens and die without going to confession actually go to eternal damnation while their likewise sinful teen friends, who went to confession before dying, go to eternal salvation? Mercy vs. Justice??
>
> Can a priest really forgive sins?
>
> Do we sin mortally if we sleep in on Sunday rather than go to Mass?
>
> Do hell and the devil really exist?
>
> How do we know the Christ/God rose from the dead?

What about the veracity of the "divinely inspired" bible that presumably recorded all the events on which we base our Catholic beliefs? Have the "stories" changed over the years or are those stories, which often seem new, the same stories read during those many Sunday masses of my youth when, even while present, I might have been catching up on my sleep?

Are all the rules propagated over the centuries by the male leaders of the Church to be believed simply because they say so, based on their own pronouncements that the Christ/God uttered certain words that put Peter and all future popes in charge?

Regardless of how we came to the Catholic faith, will we have faith that all it teaches is true and provides the best guidance to make moral decisions during our earthly lives? Or will we find it simply acceptable to unilaterally just pick and choose which tenets to believe and attempt to follow? And will effectively following those personally accepted tenets open the heavenly gates? Never-ending, unanswered questions…

Hopefully, an ever-just and forgiving God would not permit his "doubting Thomas"creations to live forever in a "Hell."

Interesting and confusing, huh!

My discernment continues…!

Nov 1961 Weird Thoughts My deep thoughts generated by the "philosophy" courses added to my confusion and likely caused my ongoing anxiety about life and existence. Strangely, for no logical reason, I began to believe I would not live beyond the age of thirty. Coincidently, that was the age of my father at his death.

Thanksgiving 1961 Heading Home Joined by fellow students Al C, John S, and Gary M, we jumped in the '49 and headed to our hometown for Thanksgiving. Extremely cold day! 130 miles! Heater broken! Headlights failing! But we made it in time for turkey!

Mysteriously, all three fellow students chose alternate forms of transportation for their returns to school.

Dec 1961 Confused by Love My relationship with Sally was certainly being tested, and I had never disclosed Sally to Bernie nor Bernie to Sally. As my progress through college began to take longer than was in her plan, Sally's "eventually" for us began to fade from my mind. However, when I received a call that she was in the hospital, quite ill, and would like to see me, I immediately went to her bedside. Our visit was necessarily short but very warm, and when I left, I was wondering if there might still be an "eventually" for us.

(ORP man was still skeptical)

(GPA 2.71 fall 1961)

Feb 1962 Avoiding the Rules College rules, including the one regarding not having visitors of the opposite sex in one's room, were strict and overbearing, so the OEA arrangement was probably good for us. But in February 1962, after deciding we had washed enough dishes for a lifetime, we decided to move on from the OEA.

At the same time, I discovered "part-time" students had no such rules, so I changed my student status to "part-time. It also meant I would need another semester to accumulate enough credits to graduate. Problem solved! (Had the draft board become aware of this change in status, my life would have changed dramatically.)

Dave was unable to use the part-time solution, as he was in the Army ROTC program and needed to remain on his four-year schedule. However, the older, married fraternity brother again provided cover for Dave by confirming to the school that Dave continued to reside with them, as allowed by the rules.

Dave also took a job as a teller at The Central Bank. I returned to selling and polishing shoes.

Pondering the future, we left our OEA quarters and forged ahead!

(ORP man was hopeful)

Feb 1962 Great Digs Leaving the OEA required finding a new residence again. Dave and I, with three fraternity brothers, moved to a new location where daily/evening activities facilitated neither studying nor cleanliness.

Experiences gained at the new location confirmed and justified again the college's rules about the academic benefits of approved housing.

May 1962 Get the Idea! A focused reader will have noticed what I mentioned about my writing on the "Philosophy of Man" final exam the "first time" I took the class. Yes, I earned an "F" and the associated privilege, not enjoyed by most other students, of taking the course again - from a different professor, who was also a priest.

The first priest professor, a middle-aged and highly intelligent individual, was perhaps somewhat frustrated by the challenges of effectively conveying "Philosophy of Man" to students like me, as he later switched teams and married a nun who was also ready to seek a new direction. This switch in their vocations provided some sense of irony to me for my failure to understand and cope with "Essence" & "Existence".

Priest professor number two was a different sort of man who was very insightful, elderly, and apparently comfortable and secure in his choice of vocation. His insight into the nature of college students showed when Bernie and me, always desiring to be close at all times, had chosen desks next to each other in the back of the room. He quickly ordered us to move to the very front row, where he could both keep an eye on us and embarrass us with philosophical questions, followed by our lack of response, followed by his detailed explanation of the answer to the question, followed by his oft-stated, and oft-repeated-by-students, phrase: "Get the Idea!!"

I lost count of the number of times my only response to his "Get the Idea!!"questions was my complete and total blank-faced stare. However, to prove that I was not a complete fool, I recalled the difficult lesson from my "F-rated" first "Man" course. On this final exam, I wrote every word I could remember having been uttered in class during the semester, in some form of, no doubt, incomprehensible sentences, on that blue-book test paper. I refrained from my usual, principles-driven psyche's temptation to document how little I understood, still, about the "Philosophy of Man."

I joyfully earned a "C"!

I had gotten the idea!

Bernie earned an "A".

(ORP Man was evolving.)

1962 Next New Life Phase A few short months after leaving OEA, the three fraternity brothers, with whom we shared the apartment, graduated, sending Dave and me searching for new living quarters again. A friend and fellow student, Jimmy, had an apartment with an extra room, which he offered to us. Though subject to the same housing rules, Jimmy had somehow gotten his apartment on the "approved" housing list.

Bernie and I had been virtually inseparable since first meeting. Contemporaneous with my early months at the bank, Bernie had moved off-campus to approved housing next door to our new (Jimmy's) apartment. My thoughts had begun to touch on our future together. But, something happened to change those thoughts.

Perhaps my feelings were hurt when she pointed out that she was from a middle-class family, while I was from only an upper, lower-class family (knowledge she had just gained in her Sociology class and felt compelled to share with me). That hurt!

Or, perhaps it was because she owed the Navy several years' service as repayment for her college expenses and would be in the military for some time, which seemed un-attractive to me.

Or, perhaps it was just my new life phase at The Central Bank…

(ORP man wondered)

(GPA 3.0 spring 1962)

May 1962 The Central Bank Where does one begin? Experiences gained at the bank were many and new, with some potentially reducing the probability of me obtaining a college degree. The bank definitely provided an inflection point in my life.

The bank was located in "The Central," the first suburban shopping center constructed in town. It consisted of 5 levels, with bars in the lower and upper levels, a major department store in the middle level, several retail outlets spread throughout the levels, and the bank's offices in the second, third, and fourth levels. The main banking floor, with teller line, loan officers, and executive offices, was on the second level.

Exceptionally attractive women tellers (most in their mid-twenties to early forties) worked the 8 AM to 2:30 PM shift, and the exceptionally handsome guys (most in their early twenties to early thirties) worked 2:30 PM to 8:30 PM Monday through Friday. The guys also worked the 8:00 AM to 2:00 PM Saturday shift. What a really great learning environment for the guys, especially with women who were inclined to share their advanced life experiences with their younger counterparts!

I entered **Job #14** at age 20, during the spring semester of my junior year. My previous jobs as a motorcycle mechanic, a part-time shoe polisher and salesman at a major department store, and a dish washer at the OEA had definitely prepared me well for being a banker.

However, taking the job would mean, for the first time, I was committed to a regular work schedule (like a real adult), and I would never again be home for summer vacation. Thus, The Central Bank "position" would mark the beginning of a permanent disconnect from my Hometown and the start of a new life phase in Big Town. It also would mean resuming a relationship with Sally was trending unlikely.

When another opening for a teller position occurred, I sought and got the position. Training began.

Fraternity Brother Dave K (a different Dave than best friend Dave R) was the teller supervisor charged with training new tellers. Day one, standing in front of me, he opened the teller cash drawer, taking my breath away with the over $10,000 currency neatly arranged in its various denominations. He then opened the bottom drawer, displaying another $10,000 currency, neatly arranged. After recovering from the shock of seeing a virtual fortune, this poor boy was relegated to watching Dave K flawlessly perform five hours as a teller during that first day of my banking career.

On the second day of my career, I became the teller under the close supervision of Dave K.

On the third day of my banking career, Dave K wished me good luck, instructed me to make no mistakes, and virtually abandoned me. I, too, performed flawlessly!

Best training program ever!

1962 ff Blame Them (some of The Central Bank staff who impacted me) Becoming acquainted with the staff of the The Central Bank was a great developmental experience, expanding my understanding of additional types of homo sapiens, to wit:

The Secretary to the Owner, who complained she was very tired of the steak dinners she had to eat almost nightly to accommodate the Owner's schedule (unbelievable to struggling college students)**!**

The tall, thin, superbly erect, slightly older male teller, who had previously experienced the privilege of belonging to The Old Guard, marching the Tomb of the Unknown Soldier.

The Switchboard Operator, confined to a wheelchair, with the sweetest smile and personality I ever experienced.

The Auditor, also confined to a wheelchair, who was very nice and always suspicious.

The deeply tanned, young bank officer, a bachelor and supervisor of the night crew tellers, who drove his beautiful red, Triumph sports car to the beach daily before coming to work.

The deeply tanned, younger night-crew-bank-officer-in-training, also a bachelor with a beautiful red Triumph sports car, who also had an affinity for the beach.

The more mature female bank officer, living with her physician boyfriend, who gifted to me a box of his old dress shirts which, although they were slightly small, snug, and short to my wrists, I wore appreciably for the duration.

The red-faced, red-haired, male bank Cashier who, being daily pressured with many administrative issues, indiscreetly and publicly yelled at me for cashing someone's bad check and directed me to find the bad guy and collect the $17.00 (which I successfully accomplished) or look for other employment.

The young male trainee who, against instructions otherwise, repeatedly extended overdraft privileges to the shopping center's restaurant operator, who daily provided him a free lunch.

The stern manager of both day and night crew supervisors who moved his family to California for greater opportunities, only to be soon tragically killed on a busy freeway.

The egotistic ("It doesn't cost any more to go first-class!") VP of Mortgage Lending who built a very profitable business for the bank that required the bank keep an apartment for him in New York City. (Hmmm!)

The former soldier, now a teller, who occasionally "borrowed" from the cash drawer to support his gambling activities.

The young bank officer whose only job seemed to be passing out pens and other trinkets carrying the bank's logo (the future CEO of the bank, as it turned out).

Gene, my main mentor.

The were others, including a girlfriend mentioned elsewhere, but vying for the title of "most interesting and experiential" was Kay S.

1962 ff Kay S As I was becoming acquainted with co-workers at The Central Bank, perhaps the most striking co-worker was an 18 year-old, part-time college student, Kay S. Kay was a skinny, somewhat unkempt, pretty, sandy-haired blonde clerk who worked in the bank's third floor offices. She would wander unsupervised in and out of the teller line and other restricted areas, seemingly lacking any concern for the security rules, with access to all. She was kind of an earth-person, beatnik type, usually wearing floor length dresses and sandals. She also was quick of lip with everyone. I had a non-sexual attraction to her, as she was strangely interesting, and we soon became good friends.

We both enjoyed jazz and were soon found hitting the jazz joints after work (work was usually finished by 9:00 PM). Neither of us was of legal age to drink in those establishments, but Kay had many friends around town, which led to occasional nights of partying at various public and/or private venues. Thus, finding an occasional alcoholic beverage or two was not difficult.

(As is perhaps evident, this new phase in my life decelerated my pursuit of the main reason I came to Big Town, i.e., to get a college education.)

Our usual mode of transport during these evenings was Kay's 1960 Volkswagen Beetle (significantly better transportation than my vastly worn, torn, and rusty 1949 Ford). As everyone who has owned or ridden in a "Beatle" during the winter knows, it is really, really cold inside, and the windshield defroster is totally useless. Many a winter night would find us flitting from venue to venue, with Kay driving and me scraping ice from both the inside and the outside of the windshield in order to see forward, while at the same time avoiding deep breathing to prevent further icing on the inside windshield. Courageously, we battled on.

The Panther Room bar was located on the lower level of The Central. Like most of the tenants of The Central, the Panther Room had a deposit account at The Central Bank. Thus, The Central Bank and the Panther Room employees became well-acquainted with each other. A similar situation existed with the employees of the 5th floor bar, The Cimarron Room. This familiarity of the employees of all three businesses facilitated our ease of being served alcoholic beverages at both bars in spite of our under-legal-age status.

The Panther Room was small and had jazz, usually in the form of a 3 — 4 piece combo, and a dance floor. Our favorite table was in an obscure, dimly lighted corner, hopefully sufficiently distant from any authorities who might stop in checking for under-age drinkers. We started many an evening of entertainment in that corner or in the Cimarron Room, which also provided desired obscurity.

One of our evenings commenced at the Panther Room, moved to the Cimarron Room, and then to other jazz locales until we arrived at The Red Lion, in the lower level of the Colonial Hotel. That evening, Kay revealed she had had a relationship with a musician who, apparently, had fallen out of like with her. While I thought we were simply having another evening of jazz and refreshments, in reality, Kay was on the hunt for her friend/lover and found him at The Red Lion. When discord between them spiraled, I found myself with a rejected and hysterical Kay, who fell to the floor and began writhing amid the many patrons. An ambulance was called and delivered her to the County Hospital, whereupon I waited to the wee hours for her recovery and release, and then I delivered her to her residence. Another new experiential night — without academic progress!

A better night with Kay started at The Cimarron Room, where we were befriended by a British flight crew that was assigned temporarily to the local air force base. After a few cordial drinks, they invited us to the Officer's Club. Requiring appropriate attire, we first stopped at Kay's residence, where she changed into the "little black dress", which was more appropriate for evenings at the Officers Club. I was already appropriately "coated and tied" from work.

The Brits treated us royally to dinner and drinks. A band played mostly big band, forties music, and each crew member danced with Kay. Then, I danced with Kay — for both the first and the last time ever. Proving that booze and a little black dress do play tricks on the male psyche, I did experience a tempting physical attraction to Kay. I believe the Brits had the same. However, for better or for worse, the music and the night ended uneventfully, lacking further life lessons.

The Central Bank days provided many other life experiences too numerous and varied with which to bore the reader, but they certainly led to the "softening" of my relationship with Bernie.

Vis-a-vis banking, the learning experiences were quite valuable as a basis for my business career. Vis-a-vis academics, The Central Bank experiences put a real stress on my "formal" education.

But, broadly speaking, these early months at The Central Bank provided lifetime "growth" experiences and contributed vastly to my social education.

(ORP man was bewildered!)

1962 ff Supervisor's Headache Friend and landlord, Jimmy, became a teller at the bank. Now, "we were three" — three headaches, that is, for the teller supervisor.

Jimmy and I had graduated high school together. With Dave, this trio partied together and experienced Saturday morning hangovers together, much to the chagrin of our Saturday morning teller supervisor. But even in our stupors, we were quite good tellers.

And competitors! Jimmy was well-known for announcing to the long lines of customers standing at our teller windows (back then, customers did their banking in person, weekly, at the bank, instead of electronically from wherever with a cellphone) that he could do any transaction Dave and I could do, except he could do it faster and better! And, he could!

And for a $225/month full-time wage each, the bank owner put up with us, as he knew this terrific trio represented a real bargain for him!

Fall 1962 Student Transportation Adventures For an inflationary $200.00, I purchased a '50 Ford to replace the "49", which had died suddenly And before I wasted time and effort transferring parts from the '49 to the '50, the '50 died, also, leaving me to the generosity of Dave and Jimmy for transportation, an option which had its own hazards.

Dave's transportation was a rusty, old, worn and torn, red Triumph sports car. One warm summer evening, after having locked the cash in the vault at The Central Bank, we were each enjoying a beer as we merrily rode, top-down, worry-free, east on Dodge Street toward the 30th street downhill "S" curve, anticipating an Indy-car-like-thrill in his trusty two-seater, when the sound of a siren and the flashing of red lights interrupted our ecstasy.

Upon pulling us to the curb, with his flashlight glaring in our eyes, the police officer inquired as to why we would so foolishly not only be minors in possession but also be drinking while driving. Luckily, the answers that formed in our brains stayed locked behind our lips. We offered no good answers. He properly and sternly admonished us to quickly get a lot smarter if we wanted to stay out of jail, stay in college, keep working at the bank, and have any chance of gaining success in life.

After emptying the contents of our beer cans onto Dodge Street, per the wise officer's direction, he told us to "lose stupid!" and wished us a safe and fun evening. How lucky could two kids be to have been apprehended by a police officer who also knew us very well, as he was also the mall cop, usually stationed just outside The Central Bank's doors?

Whew!

The benefits of "community policing" proved invaluable that night.

Winter 1962 More Student Transportation Adventures Jimmy drove a huge, old, rusty, four-door Oldsmobile that sometime in its past had had an unfortunate incident with an unforgiving object. The resulting crumpled front fender was not a beauty mark! Regardless, the Olds provided fairly reliable transportation.

One snowy winter day, Jimmy was driving us to work. Late, as usual (and usually Dave's fault), Jimmy's slightly excessive speed — down an icy 36th street — toward a green light — at a very busy main street — became a death-defying sleigh ride when the light turned red, and the Olds, with Jimmy pumping the brakes fast and furiously, spun out-of-control toward its final destiny.

In spite of the very busy, main street cross traffic, the Olds careened — collision-free — sideways — through the intersection and up the other side on 36th street, continuing on its jingle bell, merry way!

Whew! Again!

While Dave and I experienced fear and rapid heart beats during that ride, Jimmy confessed only to "…having everything under control."

Our teller manager never knew how close he came to working three teller windows by himself that afternoon!

Months later, during the summer, I treated Jimmy to a dual ride on my motorcycle. He still talks about the harrowing ride, often on the rear wheel only, with him hanging on for dear life. Jimmy experienced the fear and rapid heart beat that day!

1962 ff Career Nearly Lost In time, after months of diligent, hard work and outstanding performance, (combined with being the then longest serving male teller), I became the night crew teller supervisor.

In reality, the teller supervisors had very little authority, but for the generous $20 per month added compensation, they did get the added duties of picking up the Saturday morning mail from the post office, scheduling other tellers, filling in for tellers at meal time or when absent, counting the vault cash, balancing each day's work, and working the cramped backroom teller desk from which certain high priority business customers picked up their needed currency and coin. Though not equitably supported with incremental compensation, the position was a career stepping stone.

My career nearly ended the Saturday morning (blame the hangover) I tried to give a $10,000 currency order to a business customer who requested and paid for only $1,000. Fortunately, in that backroom, these type transactions were processed in full view of the other business customers who were also picking up their cash orders, one of whom was quick to point out my error. Without that assistance, I might have returned to a fulfilling career polishing and selling shoes.

Dec 1962 Jim's New House Bernie and I visited Mom and stepfather Jim just before Christmas, a visit intended to allow me to say goodbye to 205 H and hello to them in their new house in a suburb.

Jim had persuaded Mom to move from her much-loved 205 H to that new house. Everything seemed normal during our visit.

(I'm sure 205's neighbors had a giant, celebratory party when we moved to "Jim's new house". For many years, they had truly exhibited great patience with the motorcycle traffic, cars parked on the front yard, and the occasional night time disturbances. A special place in heaven surely awaits them.)

Mom did not tell us during our visit that the new house had become her little "house of horrors!"

During construction Jim checked on progress virtually every evening, when he also met a divorced lady and her two kids living next door in their classic Iowa farmhouse. One thing led to another, and with Jim's new house came Mom's renewed sadness and depression.

The neighbor lady became pregnant (this marine sergeant had landed once too often!) Almost concurrently with the Christmastime move into the house of horrors, Jim and Mom agreed to a divorce, (just as our skeptical relatives had always predicted), with him keeping the new house of horrors and Mom receiving a different house of horrors — a ramshackle old house at 912 G Street.

Mom said Jim always wanted his own child, which she could not give him, and he deserved this opportunity, so she would not let Carol and me interfere with the conditions of the divorce.
,
Mom just wanted this life episode to end, and she moved into the ramshackle. Three years later, combining resources, Carol and son, Kelly, moved in with her.

Unbelievably, Jim mistook his importance to me by offering me a bedroom in his new house of horrors whenever I was in town. But not even a lifetime supply of 25-cent Birdland hot dogs with mustard could have closed that deal!

(ORP man concurred)

Dec 28, 1962 First Love - Lost I was shocked and depressed when I heard the news!!

Still attending college at the time, and in spite of exploring new female relationships, I had somehow held on to the now obviously immature belief that, someday, I would be ready to marry, and she would likely be my bride. Oh, the foolish male ego!

I had seen Sally only twice after I started at The Central Bank. First, the aforementioned time I was called to her hospital bed when she was seriously ill. The illness passed, and I did not hear from her again until she invited me to her nurses training graduation program and party.

I went and enjoyed our time together, wondering, however, why she invited me, as it seemed her close friends and fellow graduates seemed somewhat distant, perhaps wondering why I was there instead, perhaps, of the person she had been recently dating. After our warm and wonderful graduation party, we had tearfully parted, unconvincingly expressing hope for a possible future together.

I was devastated a few short months later when, with no notice to me, at Christmastime, in St. John's Church, with the wedding party decorated in joyous reds and whites, just like her two older sisters had done -

Sally had married an other!

(ORP man laughed at me!)

(GPA 2.09 fall 1962)

Jan 1963 TR5 Bought my new Triumph TR5 racing motorcycle and looked forward to the spring racing schedule.

Apr 1963 VW Beetle A frat brother purchased both of my non-operating Fords for $50 and towed them away. Thanks to a very understanding banker at another bank, I replaced them with a new, 1963 VW Beetle, an essential tool for my future growth and development.

Apr 1963 Parting Was Not Such Sweet Sorrow As my time spent with The Central Bank co-workers and other new friends began to dominate my social time, my time with Bernie lessened. I began to doubt our long-term marital potential, and I was considering whether to end our relationship.

Having not acquired the social skills (being only an upper, lower-class person) needed to smoothly and gracefully extricate myself from the situation, I did some things that were hurtful to Bernie. My neanderthal social and interpersonal skills showed themselves again.

I left town without her to attend the wedding of our good friends, Dave and Dottie (it was a long-planned trip for Bernie and me), and then I took another woman to a fraternity party, also a long-planned event for us, without so much as telling Bernie I would not be taking her.

She was a beautiful, wonderful person, and I regret having treated her so poorly.

Breaking up is so hard to do! What can you say when a love affair is over?

(ORP Man was disgusted.)

(GPA 2.27 spring 1963)

Jimmy Said Go Surprisingly, my friend, co-worker, and landlord, Jimmy, suggested it was time for me to consider finding different housing, as he now had other unspecified plans for the bedroom. (Roommate Dave, of course, had precipitated this change when he decided it would be appropriate for him to join Dottie in their own basement paradise after their wedding.)

Conveniently, fraternity brother Jon S was arranging housing for four in a decent, above-ground apartment. Jon and I joined two, non-frat-affiliated students and moved in.

(ORP man was hopeful.)

Jun 1963 New Companion I was stunned when I first saw her — a young lady with a trendy, bouffant, bleached-blonde hairstyle and a couple of sizable attributes! Carol W arrived each Friday evening at the bank to deposit her packinghouse job paycheck into her nicely growing savings account, and we would visit briefly at the teller window. Using the bank's confidential files, I had located her telephone number, called, got a date, and looked forward to a wonderful relationship.

Unbeknownst to me at the beginning of our relationship, Carol W had had a longtime boyfriend who didn't appreciate her dating anyone else. Trouble followed!

To wit, two examples follow—

Upon dropping her at home after an evening date, I noticed three men getting out of a car and approaching me in the shadows as I was backing out of Carol's driveway. Having previously learned of the boyfriend's distress at Carol's dating another, and sensing trouble ahead, and having no alternative escape route, I immediately drove toward them at speed, whence they jumped out of the way and into their car. A motorized chase began.

At a nearby busy main intersection, with concrete dividers between the lanes, they chased me down the street on one side of the dividers and back on the other side. While their huge Pontiac sedan could just about catch me when we reached the end of a divider, they couldn't keep up with my VW Beetle as I made the turn and headed in the other direction.

After the fourth try, they quit chasing, and I motored on home.

On another evening, Carol and I were just stepping out the front door of a favorite pizzaria on Leavenworth Street when we heard the sounds of very loud auto exhausts and squealing tires. A car, with the boyfriend and a mate inside, screeched to a halt in the street directly in front of us. The boyfriend emerged to assault me. Fortunately, he was quite inebriated and physically small, and effortlessly easy for me to handle.

Sensing it was the right thing to do, no doubt, the mate put him back in the car, and they departed the scene.

A date with Carol was always potentially dangerous and exciting.

Nov 22 1963 It Can't Be I walked into the Student Center after class to find a crowd huddled around the TV. JFK had been shot — and died!

Mom (and millions of others) was devastated!

(ORP man cried.)

Nov 1963 Oops! Driving home from an alcohol-free evening at the Cimarron Room, a Chevrolet sedan smashed my VW! It was not my fault!

Witnesses corroborated my statement that the Chevy had run the red light. The driver was obviously inebriated. Unfortunately, he was also a county attorney. When placing him in the squad car for transport to jail, the police said he would be ticketed for DUI. Weeks later, when I inquired of my insurance company why it was cancelling me, I learned the report filed by the police stated I was at fault for the accident.

Witnesses were not mentioned in the report and naive me did not have their names. I later discovered the police had actually given the DUI county attorney a ride to a motel, and no ticket was issued.

Life lesson, kids. Beware when you are the "little guy"!

1963 Christmas at the Bank The Central Bank Christmas parties were similar to fraternity parties but with more expensive booze. After tearing the jacket of my only suit while falling down a circular staircase at the party venue, which was located 20 miles south of town, a co-worker and I navigated a blurry trip home in my VW Beatle. Foolish! I didn't let blurry eyes prevent me from driving. Henry was extremely busy again that night!

Jan 1964 Have Mercy on Me, Please Having studied into the wee hours of the morning, I overslept my 8:00 AM final exam for a one credit hour freshman Speech class, the last credit I needed to meet graduation requirements.

After throwing myself on the mercy of the priest professor, who allowed me a make-up exam, (critiquing an audio of a Churchill speech about "something"), I received a "C" and achieved the minimum requirements for graduation!

(GPA 2.13 fall 1963)

Feb 1964 Graduation After 4½ years of skipped classes, sleeping through classes, some really hard studying, living in various vermin-infested and/or party-time residences, and maturing dramatically as a person (i.e., I could now knowledgeably order from a restaurant's menu and an alcohol drink list), graduation arrived February 1964.

Given my experience years previously with the lack of relatives responding to invitations to my high school graduation, I had not bothered to notify them of this new achievement.

The celebration was fairly muted — more of a relief than a celebration. Mom came, accompanied by an older gentlemen whom I never did learn much about and never heard of after that night.

My date for the graduation evening was Carol W. After a non-memorable, and, thankfully, short speech to the graduating class by "someone eminently distinguished", certificates authorizing the graduates to pick up their respective diplomas (as soon as all their respective fees were paid and their caps and gowns were safely returned) were given individually, along with a weak-wristed handshake, a smile, and an "atta-boy" or "atta-girl", to each graduate who made the mandatory walk across the high stage in the dismal gym, all to the subdued applause of the proud parents, friends, and relatives in attendance, all feverishly snapping pictures and rolling Super 8's.

With my certificate in hand, we four then hurried off to an intimate, celebratory dinner at the town's finest pork and sauerkraut restaurant, the Bohemian Café — a seemingly appropriate finish to a less-then-stellar college experience.

Unfortunately, none of my graduation activities were captured for future re-living through the magic of film.

Carol and I did not have a special night afterwards!

The next evening, while continuing my celebrating, Ed, the bartender at the Cimarron Room, and his girlfriend, Colleen, handed to me the one-and-only congratulatory card recognizing my college graduation. I had gotten to know them quite well from my many visits to the bar, where

Ed would often give me his "mixologist's mistakes". Ed, Colleen, a late-night female friend of theirs, and I had occasionally partied together way too many nights after the bars closed.

The front cover of the card displays a uniformed army general (presumably me) atop a horse atop a columnar base, sword held high, with the words "Someday they're going to put a Statue of You in the park...and underneath it in Great Big Letters will be an inscription..." (and opening to the inside, it continued) "... Keep Off The Grass!"

Appropriately, a pigeon sits atop the general's hat.

It certainly was a fitting conclusion to an academically undistinguished, undergraduate experience!

Not long after, Carol opted to seek greener pastures, and, years later, I heard that she and the former boyfriend (of pizzaria fame) eventually married, had three daughters, and divorced. I surely dodged a bullet there!

((2.56 undergraduate career average. Summarized? (a) It could have been much worse; or (b) What a wasted opportunity!))

(ORP man was exhausted)

1964 Expanded Refreshment Experiences After graduation and while looking forward to a challenging business career, like many a young person so situated, I increased dancing with the devil while drinking his brew.

After that eventful "Bernie" night in 1960, previously described in this memoir, under the supervision of my buddies Dave R and Don D, I had begun to increasingly enjoy the flavor of the devil's intoxicating brew. My renewed taste for beer then was now being expanded by the discovery of more fashionable, sophisticated versions of bourbon, vodka, gin, Manhattans, Old Fashions, Scotch rocks, Martinis, Gin rocks, etc. Each new discovery was experienced during happenings wherein only an overworked and ambitious guardian angel, Henry, was able to prevent my injury or death.

Memorable during this time was a short-term "romantic" experience, with a very attractive older woman, which ended promptly when I learned she was the wife of a state trooper.

My naive self should have realized she was a "Cougar" when, upon entering my VW Beetle for the first time, she asked "Do you know why these cars are called "Love Bugs"?

> **Life Lesson, Kids** - Beware very attractive, older person, romantic involvements!

(ORP man frowned.)

1964 ff Career Progression Upon graduating from college in February 1964, and having worked at The Central Bank as a teller and teller supervisor for two years, I decided to pursue a bank loan officer job The loan officers always had the best clothes, the best cars, and thus, presumably, the best salaries as compared to the other bank officers. Loaning money appeared to offer a very lucrative banking career.

The bank president offered me a job at a salary of $450/month, which was $50/month more than was paid the last graduate he had hired (so I was told). Having not received competing offers from either Bank of America or RJ Reynolds Tobacco Company (the only other companies which had given me an interview), I was happy to begin **Job #15**.

However, there were no openings in the loan departments at that time, and only one department , the Controllers Department, had requested me. The president persuaded me, since loan officers were "a dime a dozen" and good controllers were hard to find, my future prospects would be much better in the Controllers Department.

Taking into consideration that I had made some very good friendships at the bank, the Controller, Gene, seemed to be a well-respected person, the rent was due, the prices of gas, cigarettes and beer were increasing, and I had no other job offers, I accepted.

Gene was an excellent boss. He taught me a great deal about the operations side of banking and a great deal about managing difficult, interpersonal relationships. The Controller often had to remind other employees of the ethics of personal and business conduct and of how bank resources could best be allocated between legitimate, competing needs. Due to the very nature of the Controller's responsibilities, occasional disagreements between the Controllers and other bank officials occasionally occurred, but were cordially handled by Gene.

The auditor also reported to Gene, and fraud was occasionally discovered via our audit activities. Required reporting of such fraud to appropriate law enforcement officials, sadly, resulted in loss of freedom for any employee or customer involved, but catching them was actually fun and self-satisfying.

Gene had started in banking as a state bank examiner. He was very skilled, which had led him, first, to the job of Auditor at the bank, and then to the executive management job of Controller. And all Controllers need an assistant, of course, which had opened the position for me.

I learned much about the internal functioning of a bank in the 14 months I first worked for Gene. I also learned how much Gene enjoyed long lunch "hours" with other bank officers and how he managed to routinely play golf during bank time. This was possible, of course, because he had such a qualified assistant (me) tending the office.

During this time, Kay S had moved to Kansas City, Sally and Bernie had both faded into the past, Carol W had departed, and Ed and Colleen had moved to another city. Fortunately, Jackie had joined The Central Bank staff, and we developed a personal relationship. We enjoyed time together and were just having fun.

Apr 1964 A New Reality My business career was off to a great start!

Then, the draft notice came!

1964 found the United States deeply involved in the Vietnam "conflict".

As the only son of a World War II naval officer who was "Killed-in-Action," and after years of receiving periodic urgings by an uncle, who had experienced combat during WW II, to not serve, I was of a mind to avoid military service. However, the draft board declined to support my request for the "Sole Surviving Son" deferment and did not support my request for an additional college deferment based on my recent, hastily arranged, part-time enrollment in a Master's Degree program. Rather, it sent me notice to appear for a draft physical.

Many of my contemporaries had chosen to get married shortly before graduation in order to obtain a "marriage" deferment. But to me, "military combat" was enormously preferable to "marriage combat"! So, I enlisted in the US Army Reserve!

Six months of active duty training, followed by 5 ½ years of weekly meetings and two weeks of annual summer camps, sounded much better than serving two years of active duty if drafted.

Soon, thereafter, my orders arrived. I was headed to Fort Leonard Wood.

Thinking I might never see home again, I entrusted my VW beetle and my checkbook to the care and use of Jackie.

After a long night of celebrating and warm goodbyes with special friends, Jackie delivered me, hangover in head and orders in hand, at 6:00 AM, to the train station, and I was on to eight weeks of Army basic training.

Apr 1964 Basic Training Our trip to Ft Leonard Wood required a transfer to another train in Kansas City, followed by a Trailways bus ride. Upon arrival at the fort, we were joined by recruits from other locations. It quickly became apparent why the government chose this location for an Army fort — i.e., sand, hills, rocks, and trees. While even the former Boy Scouts among us could not get excited about the possibilities this combination provided, most of us recruits did get excited by all the bars and related enterprises in abundance just outside the fort's main gate!

The bus stopped at the "reception" center, and we de-boarded into a semblance of a formation. A clean-sleeved, very young soldier marched us to our new digs (a WWII era barracks), with instructions to each find a bunk. Being called a "reception" center, I expected drinks and snacks. But, it might have better been called a "deception" center, as our treatment during the 20 days we stayed there, during which we were free to roam the area, shop at the PX, purchase beer, and generally enjoy our stay, led some to mistakenly feel they were actually happy to be "…in the Army now…". Alas, the truth was soon to be discovered!

While we thought he might have some command authority over us, the clean-sleeved, very young soldier turned out to be just another new recruit waiting to be assigned to a basic training unit. His name was Jeb, and he had grown up somewhere near the fort. During the two weeks it took for the Army to issue fatigues to our group, we were allowed to keep our civvies. Jeb had somehow lost his civvies but needed civvies for a date with his hometown girlfriend. With fatigues now issued, I no longer needed my civvies. After a very short negotiation, Jeb paid me $18 for my civilian pants, shirt, shoes, socks, and jacket. I was quite happy to get rid of them, as they had acquired a quite distinct, pungent odor after 20 days of use without cleaning, and Jeb was ecstatic to have civvies for his date.

Although against orders and without a pass, Jeb somehow got off the fort (he wouldn't tell us how), took his girlfriend for a "horseback ride", and returned with a smile on his face! He obviously got much better use of my civvies than I was having!

Finally, we were ordered to pack our stuff and climb onto trucks — we were heading to our basic training units. Arriving at those barracks, we were quickly ordered into four platoons and taught how to stand at attention, in our designated positions between other anxious recruits on either side. Room assignments followed. These barracks were more like college dorms (without the fun and girlie posters), with eight recruits assigned per room. Cleaning and polishing was the next order of the day, and by dinner time, the barracks were all in pristine Army condition.

After dinner, our first day of basic training was completed with polishing of combat boots and brass. Friendships were forming. Morale was high and expectations were positive. Lights out at 10:00 PM. So far, so good!

5:30 AM the following morning (my god, what are they thinking!), the sound of alarms ringing abruptly woke us. 10 minutes to formation. Fall out! Here we go — welcome to the real army! Meet your trainers. Our company's trainers included a staff Sergeant and a Corporal, both having experienced Vietnam combat more than once. Tough guys, especially the Sergeant, a short, red-headed, no nonsense career soldier. Everything by the book! No variations! Head up, shoulders back, chest out, stomach in, feet at 45 degrees with heels touching! Uniforms clean, pressed, polished - by the book! (Can I take 6 months of this? Reminded me of mandatory ROTC for 2 years at college, where egotistic, self-important student officers often abused their leadership authority. Hated that, too!)

Remember I mentioned the good days at the "deception" center? Remember they included shopping at the PX? Most recruits purchased zipper bags in which to store their purchases and, later, their civvies. First order of day two was to send home those zipper bags and the items contained therein, as they were unauthorized during basic training. Each bag was tagged with a railroad express shipping tag, and the Sergeant and the Corporal collected $3 per bag to pay for shipping. All tagged bags were then loaded into army trucks for delivery to the railroad express station to be sent home. Interestingly, the bags never arrived home, but Sarge explained it wasn't important enough to worry about right now.

Eight weeks of basic training followed, filled with marching, shooting, field life, inspections, polishing, grenades, hand-to-hand, kitchen duty, physical conditioning, grounds cleaning, and discipline. Admiration for our trainers and their knowledge and skills grew. Our company's recruits were mostly enlisted reservists and national guards. Draftees were a small percentage. As a result, our average IQ level was generally higher than that of most other companies. That level of intelligence was, I think, reflected in the progress we made with training and the lack of any serious disciplinary problems during our tenure.

Daily mail call was especially important and great for morale. We shared each other's joy or sorrow, depending on the news. Most fun for me was the correspondence from The Central Bank staff, written on a thirty-foot-long piece of two-inch wide adding machine tape.

Early in the training, I developed severe blisters on both feet, prompting the Sergeant to offer me "truck duty". Sounded great until I learned it also included kitchen duty. My days started earlier and ended later than for those recruits who were blister-free.

Finally, graduation arrived.

Every graduation required a review of the troops by the Fort's command staff. We did well! After the parade grounds review, picture taking, receipt of honors (sharpshooter for me), and return to barracks, we had only a "wake-up" to go but first needed to finish barracks cleaning and turn-in our rifles. Because some soldiers were very appreciative of our trainers for their training expertise and leadership, some soldier decided that each rifle, which had to be spotless in order to be turned in, would pass inspection only if $1 accompanied it. The funds were to go to the Sergeant and the Corporal to demonstrate our appreciation for their leadership.

I was grossly offended! Being charged any amount to turn in my rifle was against my fundamental principles, and I felt appropriate action should be taken! I complained to the company executive officer (a short, fair-skinned, red-headed 2nd lieutenant from Cedar Rapids, Iowa, whom I had gotten to know personally, as he had been occasionally called upon to lance my blisters). One thing led to another, and I soon found myself in an otherwise empty latrine, face-to-face with a now red-faced, hot-headed, vocally threatening Sergeant. Apparently, the company XO blamed the Sergeant for the fundraising scheme and threatened him with a loss of rank and income. Sarge then blamed me for his predicament.

With blunt Army verbiage, Sarge informed me, should I wish to pursue my complaint, a hearing would likely be scheduled two to four weeks hence, and I would likely be restricted to base until such hearing was completed, thus being unable to receive my much needed two week leave before advanced training started. He also opened his wallet to show me he had only $1, not the many dollars collected from the other soldiers. He offered, and I took, the $1. Case closed. My principles sold for $1! "One-dollar-Sarge" had beaten me!

Interestingly, the next morning as we were preparing to be dismissed for our two-week leave, army trucks arrived and unloaded all the zipper bags that had been collected at the start of our training. Remember, those were the bags for which each soldier paid $3 to have shipped home. One-dollar-Sarge and the Corporal blamed the express company for having failed to deliver the bags as instructed, and rather than refund the $3 fee, it had returned the bags. How naive did they think these so recently appreciative recruits could be?

My very fundamental principles were once again grossly offended, but this time, I said nothing. I had not purchased a zipper bag while in the deception center, having had nothing to put in it because Jeb had purchased my civvies, so I had no skin in this game.

I headed home for two weeks of fun and frolic. Though it was hardly enough time to visit all family and friends, it was still very much enjoyed.

Aug 1964 Advanced Training At a time when the conflict in Vietnam was intensifying, there apparently was a critical shortage of clerk/typists. Thus began the next step in my distinguished military career.

Following orders, I returned timely to the barracks at Ft Leonard Wood for Clerk/Typist School. Things I learned during those next 8 weeks—

— I could type 32 words per minute (adjusted for errors);

— Some soldiers are not happy in the Army;

— Never write anything on your Army-issued week-end pass; and

— With the proper motivation, a soldier can drive from Ft. Leonard Wood, Missouri to Rapid City, South Dakota, round tripping in 36 hours from noon Saturday to midnight Sunday.

The Clerk/Typist training center barracks were located in an old part of the fort. Thus, the barracks were also old — WWII style — , including showers for ten and toilet stools, elbow to elbow, for eight. While our new trainers worked on organizing our company and assigning barracks, we troops were kept busy the traditional Army way — senselessly moving rocks from one pile to another or policing the grounds for discarded cigarette butts and other unsightly debris. While diligently avoiding finding any butts or other debris, I began getting acquainted with my fellow clerk/typist trainees and generally discussing how we could minimize our efforts during the upcoming eight weeks of training. This strategizing was interrupted when I received an order to report to the company headquarters.

I'd been there less than eight hours! What could I have possibly done wrong so quickly? Did my beloved and admired basic training Sergeant communicate with my new clerk/typist training Sergeant about my principles? Would I have to pay $1 to turn in my typewriter at the end of training?

NO! It was something much worse!

Upon reporting to HQ, and without fanfare, my new training Sergeant threw a trainee's three-stripe arm band to me, telling me I was now in charge of, and responsible for, my barracks and my 39 fellow clerk/typists-in-training. I had been looking forward to maintaining a very low, no pressure profile. Now I was going to have responsibilities! Not what I had had in mind!

Why me, Lord? Seems new Sarge had read my paperwork and discovered I had satisfactorily completed two years of Army ROTC in college, thus apparently qualifying me to be the "leader of the clerks."

New Sarge also chose four other clerks to be squad leaders under my command. They each received two-stripe arm bands to demonstrate their command responsibilities. So, the platoon leadership team was set — five clerk leaders, all reservists, whose primary wish in life until several months ago was to avoid military service and, subsequently, to never bear the heavy responsibilities being suddenly thrust upon us.

Basic training had instilled a discipline in us that rewarded those who followed the directions of their leaders, so the rest of the first day went well. The barracks were cleaned and personal belongings and uniforms were properly arranged. We were prepared for the first inspection, scheduled for the next morning. Morning came. Inspection was passed. Morning chow was devoured, and off we went, marching in formation a mile to the typewriter training huts. Everything was proceeding as planned. Our platoon leadership team was doing well!

Then, the challenges to leadership began! A stocky Italian from Chicago, claiming to "have connections", decided his personal hygiene routine would include a wet shower followed by a huge dusting of talcum powder followed by a sunbath sans clothing next to the barracks and in sight of HQ. My repeated admonitions to his squad leader failed to resolve the problem (even on an all-male army base, certain activities are frowned upon), so extra restrictions for the "connected" Italian and a replacement for the squad leader solved the problem. Original squad leader #1 had failed command responsibilities.

Two weeks into training, an original squad leader decided he no longer would participate in the required barracks cleaning, abandoning his duties to his troops in favor of a night at the PX bar. When he returned, he preferred to fight rather than clean. At the hands of several clerk/typists, he received a shower (without talcum) and an escort to his bunk. Too bad! I had had great hope for the leadership he could provide. Squad leader #2 failed his command responsibilities and was replaced.

The third and fourth original squad leaders simply asked to be relieved — the responsibilities were too great, and they were not making any friends. Squad leaders #3 and #4 failed and were replaced.

Week-end Relief—

The best part of Advanced Training was definitely the week-end pass.

We were allowed off-base passes, restricted to a short distance from the fort. On several week-end passes, I traveled beyond the allowed distance from the fort. One such week-end was spent in Kansas City, where Kay S then lived. We spent an evening visiting several jazz venues. Great time! However, when using a Kansas City telephone book to locate her, I had written her telephone number on the only piece of paper available at the moment — my Army week-end pass.

When I returned to the fort Sunday evening, I deposited my pass, as required, at company HQ and hit the sack. The next morning, I was ordered to HQ and learned, unequivocally, that one does not "deface" government property by writing on the pass! I nearly lost my three stripes and privileges over that misstep.

During most of the 36-hour weekends, several of us traveled together to our respective homes, which were even further from the fort than was Kansas City. One of the clerk/typists-in-training kept his car parked outside the fort and would drop four of us at our homes as he continued to Rapid City, where he would spend a few hours with his girlfriend before starting the return trip.

Riding with him was harrowing, as he would not allow anyone else to drive. It was all we could do to keep him awake on the trips back. Fortunately, we survived.

Somehow, I also survived the eight weeks as the platoon leader. I suppose I could attribute my personal leadership success to my strong management and human relations skills accumulated through prior experiences in Boy Scouts and business, but it's also possible the clerks were just easy to lead and only wanted to get through training, graduate, and go home. Maybe it was dumb luck. Maybe Divine Providence. Maybe some of each.

At the end of eight weeks, all platoon members passed their final exams and graduated. I had become a certified Army-trained, 32-word-per-minute (adjusted for errors) Clerk-typist, punching three wpm fewer than before my Army training! With Clerk/typist school successfully behind me, I turned in my stripes and headed home to Jackie and my job at The Central Bank.

As her home was directly on my path home. I called Bernie and asked if I could stop and visit with her. She declined my offer and abruptly ended my telephone call.

Who would have guessed…!

1964 Early Arrival Fort Leonard Wood soldier buddy from Rapid City announced arrival of their first child, a daughter, born somewhat prematurely. All were doing fine.

1964/65 Moving on Up Returning to my job at The Central Bank, Jackie and I resumed our personal relationship, and she returned my VW and my checkbook — both intact.
I also reunited with Jon S, my frat brother, in another rented house — perfect for bachelors.

Eight months later, in a surprise to all employees, the bank's owners sold the bank to a large, multi-bank holding company headquartered in "Big City" in another state.

Almost immediately after the sale was completed, I was offered a position at the holding company. Feeling coerced by my boss and mentor, Gene, under his threat of firing me if I passed this opportunity, I finally accepted the job, loaded my VW with "all" my belongings (except the stereo system, which Jackie took to her house for safekeeping) and celebrated July 4,1965 on the road, headed to **Job #16,** my new "executive position".

My next life phase of exceptional growth was beginning!

Jul 1965 ff Darrell's House Upon arriving in "Big City", I bunked with my new boss, Gene F, while searching for permanent living quarters. He, being a particularly persnickety person, assisted me in quickly finding a place to live — a house owned by "Darrell" and occupied by Darrell and his two roommates. During the course of my 19 months in Big City, there were as many as five of us occupying Darrell's three bedroom house — perfect for bachelors in their youth.

The very first morning after I moved in, I was "shocked" to discover an attractive young woman with long black hair, partially clothed in a white fish-net "sleeping" garment, arising out of the sofa sleeper bed in the living room, followed immediately by Darrell. After a brief introduction, she left, not even staying to enjoy the excellent breakfast Darrell then prepared.

My job required travel, leaving my bedroom empty through the week. That was when a 5th roommate joined us, and I was moved into a bedroom shared with Darrell. This was a very small house, so bedroom space was tight and not very comfortable, but for the reduced rate of $20 per month, who was I to complain.

Darrell's house was the party house of the neighborhood. I don't know what happened during the work week, as I was usually on the road, but the weekend parties were frequent and quite sophisticated. Darrell was a master chef. Dinner often included a beef tenderloin roast prepared on the grill, with Coquilles St. Jacques in a pastry shell (both new gastronomical experiences for me) and/or shrimp cocktails and, of course, the finest alcohol drinks. Most partiers were couples from the neighborhood and/or some imported young ladies from beyond the neighborhood's borders. Music and crazy dancing would follow until the wee hours.

Denis W, a college acquaintance whom I had bumped into when working an assignment in Fargo, ND, joined us on occasion when he traveled through town. He thoroughly enjoyed our hospitality. (In the future, Denis became much like the brother I never had).

If the party wasn't at our house, we would enjoy an evening of drinking and dining out on the town. A favorite place for hors d'oeuvres and drinks was "The Apartment," located on the lower level of The White House restaurant. Loosely modeled after The Playboy Club, the lady servers were attractive, and the food and drink were exceptional — all accompanied by extraordinary piano jazz.

Sep 1965 ff Representing the Home Office My first assignment on my new job at the home office in Big City was to lead a two-month project at an affiliated bank in Great Falls, Montana. The first evening there, a group of the bank's employees invited me to join them at an employee's home, after we had already consumed serious cocktails at The Red Door bar. It was probably a grand party, but the only person waking the next morning, on the employee's home basement floor, was the guy from the home office. Certainly embarrassing!

1965 ff Female Overload Big City women were quite aggressive.

On one of our many evenings out together, roommates Darrell, Bob, Bill, and I ventured into an enormous roadhouse bar which had a very loud rock band and many more girls than guys — an uncharacteristically wild venue for us older "sophisticates". Finding open seats at a group table, and upon their invitation, we joined some young ladies and shouted introductions. Sitting next to one of the ladies, in astoundingly short order, I realized she was becoming much more physically acquainted with me than should ever happen after such a short courtship. What a learning experience!

My department's secretary was likewise aggressive. Accepting an invitation to her apartment was, well, interesting. Surrounded by dark woodwork, candlelight, a flickering fireplace, with luscious food and alcohol drinks served, she was a more than generous hostess. Such entertaining evenings abruptly ended after several weeks, however, after she began speaking about our future together!

I met two particularly attractive young women who had first become acquainted with Darrell and had accepted his invitation to a Saturday morning breakfast at our house. Scandinavian beauties, Idele and Sharon were sisters who came from a small, rural town to experience life in Big City. Although I was initially attracted to the brunette, older sister, Sharon, I soon found Idele, the beautiful blonde with the pony tail reaching down to her lower back, was drawing my attraction.

The sisters frequented our parties and hosted us at their apartment. Their father had gifted them a new, 1966 Plymouth convertible, which made them even more attractive (we assumed father had some big bucks). Our occasional dates out with the sisters were group dates, with Darrell escorting Sharon and me with Idele. As much as I tried to intensify my relationship with Idele, it remained in the "good friends" stage. I treated Idele with great respect, but to no avail.

Big City was fun and a great learning experience. My weekly work travel to exotic places like Mankato, Minnesota, Great Falls and Helena, Montana, Bismarck and Minot, North Dakota, and Omaha and Hastings, Nebraska, during my 19 months employment in Big City, made me somewhat travel weary. I hated to leave, but with a great new job opportunity, and having made little romantic progress with Idele, it was time.

After a very cold February 1967 day of snow-sledding with the neighbors and their kids, I packed my few belongings into my exceptionally cool, studded-tired, 1966 Mustang GT (the VW replacement) and headed to a new job back in Big Town.

Feb 1967 Moving on Up Again Though I thoroughly enjoyed my life in Big City, I couldn't decline the new job opportunity.

My former boss and mentor, Gene B, had taken a promotion to a larger bank owned by the same holding company, and he needed an assistant. So I returned to Big Town, from whence I had come.

A few months later, an acquaintance at The Central Bank gave me a newspaper clipping of Idele's wedding, where she had become "Mrs. Petersen". She also informed me the Petersen's were the proud parents of a newly (and "prematurely") born child.

To this day, I don't know how that acquaintance was aware of my interest in Idele, or how she apparently kept that knowledge to herself, as it was well-known within The Central Bank staff that I was, and had been for the entire time I was in Big City, also actively enjoying my relationship with Jackie. Jackie never asked me to explain.

Small world! Impossible to keep a secret!

Feb 1967 Job #17 required long hours and hard decisions for Gene and me, but he still found time for golf during business hours. How did he find the time???

I also again joined Jon S, who was now in law school, in a rented house, perfect for bachelors. George W, a new friend, made us a threesome. Broncos cheeseburgers, fries, and Hamm's beer were usually on the dinner menu.

Great fun always followed.

(ORP man was holding on tight)

1967 Really? I just received notice from my draft board. They had reconsidered and reclassified me "Sole-Surviving-Son" and appropriately provided a deferment from military service.

Timely?? I did not respond to the draft board, as I preferred to finish my six-year US Army Reserves commitment as agreed.

1967 ff Not-Yet-DW Very early in my return, I had concluded that it was unfair to Jackie to continue our relationship as, after extensive consideration, I realized I was not ready for marriage nor for a long-term, non-marital relationship. I was clearly committed to concentrating on my business career.

A very difficult discussion was had.

Breaking-up is so hard to do! Nothing sweet about it!

Weeks later, and fully unanticipated, I developed a yearning for an attractive young lady who was working in another department at the bank.

Coffee breaks in the bank's very small lunch room provided up-close, much appreciated viewing of co-workers, especially for the men when the female co-workers passed from the coffee service window to their usual tables. Some of the younger, less-refined male employees would go so far as to group-rate each female on a one-to-ten scale, a process eventually and immediately discontinued when the bank CEO became aware. One special young lady, referred to here as "Not-Yet-DW", rated a ten, and we soon began dating.

Change comes so fast, sometimes like an earthquake! I began pondering if I was ready for a major life style change!

(ORP man was hopeful)

1967 Oops! With roommates Jon and George as passengers, on what was now becoming a much less frequent night out with the boys due to my now more frequent nights out with "Not-Yet-DW", and after multiple toasting to the benefits of "bachelorhood" at several locales, a galvanized metal power pole suddenly jumped in front of my "Ultra cool, 1966 Mustang GT". and my "Ultra cool, 1966 Mustang GT" suddenly became simply "wrinkled 1966 Mustang GT".

Fortunately, the pole tumbled, and we three and the wrinkled one moved on without looking back.

Foolishly, the evening's festivities continued, and Henry and his two co-workers were kept very busy. They did an excellent job!

Sep 1967 Cold Turkey Though the R.J. Reynolds Tobacco Company will surely regret this particular evening due to the negative financial impact on them of me quitting my three-pack-a-day habit of smoking Camels - the original, unfiltered type - I quit cold turkey!

As I had smoked my last Camel earlier that evening, Gene E gave me one of his Pall Malls — my last smoke — which I thoroughly enjoyed as I relaxed, late at night, in bed, prior to sleep.

Quitting was pursuant to a group of four bank officials wagering $100 each about who could quit smoking from September 13, 1967, until January 1, 1968. All four quit, so no one had to pay, but Gene B, Dick S, and John N each resumed smoking on January 1.

My lungs began to clear. My clothes and my fingers no longer suffered burns or yellow stains.

A non-smoker, Not-Yet-DW was especially pleased!

Dec 1968 Not-Yet-DW After an appropriate period of dating, discussions of marriage began. At the time, I was seriously considering accepting a job offer with an international bank in New York City — a fabulous career opportunity! Alternatively, we could marry and settle in Big Town.

Choices, choices! Decisions, decisions!

After consuming sufficient Manhattans in a dark, secluded corner of a cocktail lounge, I proposed! She accepted! Another Friday night crazy!

(ORP man smiled)

Dec 1968 Maturing? I traded my wrinkle-repaired, ultra-cool, 1966 Mustang GT for a 1968 Ford Galaxie 500 "family" sedan.

(ORP man smiled again)

Mar 1969 Pre-Marital Disaster So, it began. Announcements to the world; congratulations received; parent-sponsored engagement party with the relatives; wedding plans formulated; invitations ordered; church and reception facility reserved; pre-Cana completed. But, suddenly, I became seriously uncomfortable with the very real, looming prospect of another significant life change.

Not-Yet-DW was all that I desired in a wife: same religion, great family background, cute, funny, smart, an excellent kisser, passionate. Why my discomfort? Perhaps the primary reason a nearly 28 year-old bachelor fears marriage —it is hard to give up the self-determination of the bachelor life for the challenges and responsibilities of the married life.

So — engagement broken!

Not-Yet-DW took a job elsewhere (a local top-50 radio station staffed with many "wild and crazy" DJ personalities); sold her Dodge Dart and bought a rad, blue Camaro with white leather interior (using her wedding savings), and terminated our contact. The priest, who had conducted our pre-Cana sessions, offered Not-Yet-DW counseling, suggesting she and he trip to San Francisco for respite. Not-Yet-DW's cousin, Nancy, pestered me relentlessly about what a huge mistake I had made.

So much to consider...

And I was in deep reflection on it all!

(ORP man was disgusted)

Jun 1969 Recovery Within weeks, Not-Yet-DW and I reunited.

A new, expedited wedding date was set (our need for speed thoughtfully questioned by those suspicious). The original date was crossed out on the invitations; the new date was written in; all details were hurried; and a young girl's dream of the perfect wedding was, sadly, dashed!

Wedding was held in Not-Yet-DW's church. Both the men and the women in the wedding party performed marvelously in their fast-found, ill-fitting, off-the-rental rack wedding garb. The photographer arrived late, failing to capture on film some memorable moments. Not Yet-DW experienced extreme anxiety, justifiably concerned that her prince might not appear.

Best friend Dave was best man. Not-Yet-DW's sister, Linda, was maid of honor. Best friend, Carma Jean, and cousin, Nancy, were bridesmaids. Also present were our families, friends, and my former roommates from Big City and locally.

Sighs of relief were heard throughout the crowd when the "I do's" were finished. Not-Yet-DW had become, simply, DW, and she sighed her own resounding relief. I was still perspiring.

A small crowd reception was held in the church's drab school lunchroom. Cold cuts, beer, and cake were served; and it was over - June 7, 1969.

Then we were off in DW's rad, blue Camaro with white leather interior, on a three-day honeymoon, stopping day-one at a Holiday Inn honeymoon suite (brightly decorated in joyous reds and whites, with a complimentary, off-year liter of champagne served in matching souvenir glasses), and day-two at a similar motel near where I had lived in Big City. As anticipated, DW really had no need for all 19 pairs of shoes that filled her rad Camaro's trunk.

With the honeymoon over, we hurried back home to our little, basement-level apartment love nest.

Years of "getting acquainted" had begun!

(ORP man was overjoyed)

1969 Global Surprises 1969 was a year of global surprises. Woodstock happened; Vietnam troop withdrawal began; ARPANET communications emerged; earthlings walked on the moon (or did they?); and I was learning Marriage 101 in a basement-level love nest with DW, my beautiful, young and talented bride!

Jun 1969 Another Bachelor Transitions Cohort in mischief, Denis W, married Marian two weeks later, dangerously reducing the world bachelor population by one more.

1969 ff Fred and CJ Immediately began a close friendship with Fred and Carma Jean. DW and Carma Jean were best friends from kindergarten. She and Fred, a neighborhood boy who had won Carma Jean's heart, had married right after high school and soon had their son, Scott.

We were often included in Fred and Carma Jean's business and social activities. Fred was successful in his advertising career, and they eventually moved to California and started their own business. Years later, we were pleased when they returned to Big Town and enhanced our social lives again.

Mar 1970 Military Obligation Completed! Although offered a third stripe for re-upping, I opted for no more weekly meetings and summer camps. Six years was sufficient. I am glad to have had the Army experience, even though it was relatively subdued. Some soldiers become heroes. Some die in service. Some live to enjoy the rest of their lives and quietly pass. Some cannot escape the horrid experiences they have witnessed.

I wouldn't trade it for anything, but I don't wish to repeat it, either.

While I grew up thinking I would never serve, I'm proud that I did. I also pray for those who served but never returned.

(Note: Thankfully, I never was assigned a Clerk/typist job during my six-year Army career!)

1970/1971 Forced to Relocate DW and I escaped our "first-year-of-marriage, basement-level love nest" to a nice upscale, above-ground-level apartment. After this apartment was broken into during our third month of occupancy, we escaped again to a really upscale, ground-level apartment (i.e. a "ghost" magically picked up our garbage from a kitchen pass-through door, and we were allowed the use of two garages for the price of one), but we were forced to leave our "Camelot" after one year, as children were verboten (a family of three was on the horizon).

(ORP man was excited)

1971 Marital Mountains and Molehills A throat-swelling attack that occurred shortly after we were married took me to an allergist, who concluded, after running a multitude of grossly expensive tests, I should avoid dirt, mold, and Kleenex. Though much more expensive than that of Dr. Noun, the allergist's advice was much less valuable!

My self-diagnosis theorized the possibility of a cause/effect relationship with the "early-in-the-marriage, bachelor-to-husband, domestication program."

As I continue my lifetime effort to chill (i.e.,chuckle and smile) in response to any of the frequent "disasters of daily living", so as to minimize the possibility of warming saliva, throat-swelling, and widely expanding bodily hives, DW, who often reacts to any such "disasters" as being of "world-stop-turning" significance (e.g., "I'm below 1/2 on gas!"), considers my chilling to be simply an irresponsibly slow and passively non-interested concern

As a result, my "in good time" response to such disasters rarely satisfies her need for "now!", and my molehills quickly become my mountains, also, and require "now" action.

So we do have our "days", but, happily, with the advice I received from Alfred E. Neuman and Dr. Noun, all disasters are eventually resolved without a trip to the ER.

So lift your glasses to my advisors Alfred E. Neuman and Dr. Noun. May they reign forever!

Dec 1971 Best Thing Ever! Our favorite child, a daughter, was born December 28, 1971, and we welcomed her to our first "owned" house.

Becoming ill at the hospital while awaiting her birth, I returned home immediately after, leaving DW and our newborn child alone. DW, weeks after coming home with our daughter, took three well-deserved days leave with her sister for R&R in Denver.

Three days with an infant were still challenging for me, but both father and daughter somehow survived.

1975 A Good Man I finally met my new brother-in-law, Ron S. Our initial conversations disclosed we had both experienced some of the same people, places , and saloons during our respective job-related travels in the upper mid-west states. I anticipated we would have some good times together in the future!

1975 A Good Team Over the previous eight years, with Gene B's leadership, we achieved significant improvements in the internal accounting, operations, and administrative functioning of the bank, and we were rewarded with appropriate promotions and compensation.

In 1975, Gene, then a Senior Vice President and Cashier, and an executive officer of the bank, accepted a promotion to a position in Big City with the holding company, and I was promoted to his vacated position. More hard work and rewards followed.

DW was very pleased!

1975 Spending Time at the Library (but don't tell the boss) On another Friday night, shortly after my promotion to the Senior Vice President position, several co-workers and I stopped at a bar for discussion and refreshments. The discussions continued well into the evening.

My next memory was of one of the aforementioned co-workers waking me early the following morning, sun shining brightly, from a deep, alcohol-induced sleep, in the front seat of my 1968 Ford Galaxie 500 family sedan, windows down with feet protruding, parked in the lot behind the downtown library. DW had been frantically calling my co-workers to determine why I had not returned home the previous evening and search parties had been scouring the city.

Being vulnerable, as I was, to various acts of violence at night in the downtown area, my evening could have been terminal.

Thankfully, dear, dear Henry was there!

1975 ff Enlightened Management Skills During my time as Senior Vice President, I continued to study management techniques, and I adopted several methods, designed to improve operating results, that were foreign to the rest of the bank's managers.

One of these techniques was my approach to the annual job performance reviews.

I tended to concentrate on subordinates' achievement of results, rather than just the mostly subjective, qualitative traits listed in the HR performance forms, so I designed and added "results vs. goals" forms to the review package. Using both formats, my strong performers would then receive excellent or above average ratings, while my poor performers would receive average ratings. However, poor performers would also receive a personal letter from me regarding any uncorrected issues still needing their attention . These letters were not copied to the HR Department for entry into their "permanent" records, as I realized my analysis of their performance could possibly be unfairly destructive of their future opportunities within the organization. I simply hoped these personal letters would help them improve their performance.

In all cases, a face-to-face discussion followed.

It seemed to be effective, as most subordinates blossomed, and I had to terminate only one subordinate during my tenure.

Another technique was to request subordinates to write an honest review of my job performance. Of the six managers reporting directly to me in 1977, only Tony P took advantage of that opportunity.

Tony was brutally honest. Some of his comments —
- will accomplish an objective at any cost
- creates self-doubt in subordinates by lack of compliments and thoughtless remarks
- uncanny ability to become involved in everything but only those in which he is interested
- reacts after hearing only one side of the story
- too intent, will self-destruct
- robs his family of his own time

He gave me an overall rating of "average" on the HR form, with a note suggesting specific steps I should take to improve my performance.

He delivered his comments only in writing - exiting quickly. I appreciated his truthfulness and accuracy (though he made no comments on my quantitative results vs. goals), and I subsequently tried to improve my approach to management accordingly.

I believe my approach to "results vs. goals" performance reviews, supplemented with the personal letter when needed, produced better communication and less animosity than the HR-only process. As for a subordinate reviewing the boss' performance, it also works wonders.

His performance review of me was, thankfully, not copied to the HR Department!

1976 Rewards of Leadership Leadership carries a burden of uncertainty — not always knowing whether your decisions will prove to be correct; whether your boss believes in you; whether your team supports your decisions. Whether a project succeeds or fails doesn't alleviate that uncertainty. Reassurance comes occasionally from meaningful feedback, such as a note I received from the newly-widowed spouse of a respected subordinate:

"Thanks. Berkley always appreciated and respected you!"

No expression of support could have been more rewarding .

1977 Feeling Guilty I vaguely recollect another Friday evening, probably much like the "Library Parking Lot" evening, which started with after-work refreshments and continued much too long, when I may have backed my 1968 Ford Galaxie 500 family sedan's enormous chrome rear bumper into the side of someone else's automobile.

Although I'm still not sure it actually happened, nor when or where it might have happened, the possibility that it happened resides in my sub-conscience and periodically emerges to cause me great anxiety. Could I have caused great property loss to someone? Was I guilty of a "kiss-and-run"? Will I soon be arrested and lose my job, family, and future?

Or was this merely a dream, much like the one in which I killed someone? This I must investigate and make amends.

Henry, can you help?

1978 Another Friday Night I was blurry-eyed driving home in the bank president's beautiful, black 1975 executive Chevrolet Caprice (a grand car with all the extras) when I suddenly realized I was driving in a roadside ditch rather than on the street. I gave Henry another huge challenge that night. Praise to you, Hank!

Henry and I would have been much better off if weeks had only six nights (no Fridays - except that one in the secluded corner of the bar, of course)!

1978 Passion of Youth Nephew Kelly had grown and matured into a 19 year-old who adored a 17 year-old neighborhood missy, Janise. A wedding followed, and they moved to their own rented love shack — a very small trailer house equipped with a water bed that barely fit within. Their new adventure had begun.

1979 A Sudden Awareness My skeptical belief and/or analytical inquiry in so many tenets of the Catholic Church began in college. Still, I was so proud and reassured when watching my eight-year old daughter process in her white, First Communion gown and headpiece.

But, my discernment continued...

Aug 1979 We moved into a very nice, new home (our third owned residence), in a choice, upscale neighborhood, anticipating an even better future. Life was good.

DW rejoiced!

(ORP man relaxed)

1979 Hank vs The Devil's Brew After pondering for some time whether I had a "problem," I eventually recognized that not only did I have a problem, but we were also creating a problem for our eight-year-old daughter, who was joining DW and me for our nightly, after-work routine of enjoying a cocktail or glass of wine.

She would pull her chair next to ours and enjoy her Shirley Temple kiddie cocktail. It took this sledge hammer observation for me to finally recognize how far down the wrong track I had gone.

Overnight, I became alcohol-free.

Then, looking back with a clear head, I realized my guardian angel, Hank, had held me in his protective arms many, many times.

Without the protection of an overworked guardian angel, my life would have been much different. Though this is not intended as a testament to the reality of guardian angels, I'm confident Hank is real and saved me many times from losing everything I held dear.

I hope my **young readers** will heed **lifelong lessons** I learned from my experiences with Hank and the Devil's brew.

I stress to my young beginning imbibers to beware, so they don't, like me, become unable to handle alcohol properly.

And even though DW says I was more fun when I was imbibing, Hank and I will continue happily on our alcohol-free journey.

(ORP man was overjoyed)

1980 Stepfather I learned today that, although former stepfather Jim had had several years with his new wife, new house, new child, and two new stepchildren, he suffered from various diseases in his later years. He died August 12, 1980, seventeen years after the divorce, at the age of 48 — of complications from diabetes.

He did enjoy those sundaes and sodas!

1969/1981 Synopsis of Married Life So Far The training program for new husbands can be long and hard! DW seeks "perfection" in all things, while I seek only "good enough". She is "form and function," while I am mostly "function." Our contrasting focuses have come to be known, respectively, as "OCD" and "half-assed". OCD usually wins all debates (girls rule)!

I learned my Sicilian/Irish wife has a scary dark side, supported by the large population of Sicilian relatives in town. She early warned me, if I ever fooled around with another woman, she would know, and I would never sleep peacefully thereafter. Charming, as always!

A devout practitioner of sarcasm, she excels! Among her favorite names for me, which she proudly shares with acquaintances, are "Al" and "SFB". "Al" is for "Alzheimers" and "SFB" is for "S_ _ t for Brains". Oh, the love!

Marriage so far had featured both wonderful and less-wonderful experiences, with DW becoming firmly in control. The "perfect corporate wife", as she was once labeled by a new social acquaintance even though DW often told such new social acquaintances that I was a chicken-boner at the local processing plant. She always made me look good, and as we edged into mid-life, DW guided our health options, requiring appropriate exercise routines and replacing our tasty, high caloric food choices with decidedly less tasty, healthy food (but retaining occasional dark chocolate and red wine for herself).

DW is very social and talks to everyone. It had become our preference, when dining out casually, to take our places at the bar, facilitating lively conversation with both the bar staff and other patrons. Such evenings often ended with DW offering a substantial and protracted goodbye hug for whomever had become our newest acquaintances and/or excessively tipping the bartender who gave her a "good pour."

I, on the other hand, am not a good conversationalist. I'm not anti-social; just not very social. (This may be a result of my youth, when kids were to be seen but not heard.) DW often remarks: "I live with a mute!"

So, with rare exception, I neither gave nor received a hug, and my tipping was considered "conservative"!

1981   Soured   In 1981, after six years as Senior Vice President and Cashier of this bank, and 19 ½ credited years of employment and outstanding accomplishments with the holding company, my relationship with the boss, Don M, soured, as I was feeling under-appreciated and dissatisfied with future prospects. I, sadly and foolishly, resigned from the best job ever and sought employment elsewhere.

Departure date was delayed for two months, but severance was not offered.

DW was not pleased with the news!

(ORP man sighed)

1981   Career Progression   When searching for my next career position, a member of the bank's board of directors hired me for an executive position at his grain company. Unfortunately, I realized in less than a month, **Job #18** was not a good fit. It took 18 months for the boss to agree with me. I began my job search again

Fortunately, the job had given me a great education in how corporations use huge economic power and significant financial leverage to their advantage.

Piddly severance!!!

DW was not pleased with the news!

1982   Consultant   **Job #19** was a great character-building experience.

Self-employed consultant (a/k/a having zero income), I joined two associates on a startup project for a bill-paying service which was designed to be offered by banks to consumers. The service tested good operationally, but the project was terminated when neither the banks nor ourselves had sufficient capital to continue the project during the generally poor economy.

1983   Another BIG Job   **Job #20** came when I joined Citicorp as a Vice President and managed a new banking operation, which was part of a four market national test, in Big Town. Eighteen months later, that test was discontinued nationally, and our jobs were eliminated.

Given the choice of nine months' severance pay or a Citicorp job in Tampa, Florida, I gladly accepted the nine months' pay.

I had enjoyed another invaluable learning experience!

1985 ff Job #21 Offered In 1985, Tony P (the same Tony who, as a direct report to me a few years previously had written a review of my job performance) asked me to join him at a nearby bank as Senior Vice President of Lending.

Tony knew me well from our time in Big Town, before he transferred to another bank in North Dakota, as its number two executive. He had recently joined this nearby bank as President and CEO, with the challenge of fixing its many problems.

We and our wives, DW and Margaret, were also good friends.

Having a boss who was previously a subordinate could be uncomfortable. I considered declining the offer, but the position looked promising, and I accepted.

DW was very pleased!

It took hard work and time, and with the help of a great staff, the bank was brought to good health.

Tony was a good boss, the town was good, the people were good, and the times were good.

(ORP man was pleased.)

1959/1988 Carol and Mom over the Years As these years passed, Carol progressed in her hospital administration career. Mom continued to work as a registered nurse, retiring in 1980.

Carol and Kelly lived with Mom until Carol was able to purchase her own ramshackle on 5th Ave, where she was joined for a short while by new husband Ed and his two children - until their divorce.

In time, she married a non-English speaking Greek immigrant (name not important), who departed soon after, never to be heard from again.

Over several years, both Mom and Carol improved their respective homes whenever funds allowed. In 1970, Mom sold her ramshackle and moved in with Carol and Kelly.

A number of suitors (all of whom, I suspect, had inappropriate intentions) of various pedigrees and ethnicities also floated through Carol's life and her house. Though now finished with thoughts of marriage, Carol still sought romance.

An oft recalled quote of Mom's during this period: "This is like a damned United Nations!"

As mentioned previously, Kelly and Janise married in 1978 and had moved into their own rented love shack, leaving Mom and Carol together with a sense of a job half-done.

During these years, I helped make repairs to each of the "ramshackles" when I could, usually during my summer vacations.

1988 Disabling Injury At age 48, Carol was injured while exiting her place of employment. A heavy, brass door closer fell from the door and landed on her neck, leaving her spine and surrounding nerves damaged, resulting in her being unable to continue employment at the hospital.

Subsequently, since she was experiencing continuous pain which required expensive medication, her lawyer felt she was justified in seeking compensation from her employer and the contractor whose responsibility it was to properly maintain the hospital's physical facilities. Lawsuits were filed against the hospital and the contractor, a large national corporation.

In time, the lawsuits were heard before a jury. Carol's young attorney, who had taken the case on a contingency, was adept at presenting the case. The contractor quickly felt inclined to settle and offered a $250,000 settlement. While others may have felt this offer was reasonable and would avoid the possibility of receiving nothing from a jury, Carol determined it was inadequate, and she would rather receive nothing than settle for such a "measly" sum that would do little to improve her quality of life. The case went to the jury, which shortly returned a favorable decision and recommended a substantially larger judgement. Neither the hospital nor the contractor appealed.

Upon receipt of the awarded funds, the attorney issued his trust account check to Carol, net of his 40% contingency fee. We all rushed to the attorney's bank and cashed the check. Although leaving Carol somewhat uncomfortable with only a nominal amount of pocket cash, most of the funds were immediately transferred to her new trust account and invested in various maturities of US Government treasury bills, notes, and bonds.

But before proceeding, it is well to reflect on the moment Carol, Mom, and I saw the funds actually come under Carol's control. Being relatively poor and of typical working class stature, the actual receipt of all that money was exhilarating. Recalling how our young, weekly allowances had been, on a good week, 10 to 25 cents, the thought of Carol being a millionaire was breathtaking.

Carol, of course, felt some anxiety when most of the funds immediately transferred into her trust account, as the feeling of wealth immediately became less tangible with the funds in the trust account rather than in her own checking account. In time, however, she became more comfortable with the location of those funds and the lifestyle the funds enabled.

Carol's immediate purchases included an upscale house in a suburb and a Lincoln Town Car. Most psychologically important, it was goodbye to her ramshackle! Mom and Carol moved up, and I retired as their ramshackle "DIY-er".

1993 Day Ruined! I was enjoying the best of Campbell's soup (chicken noodle and sodium) from the bank's vending machine when Sam, a tenant in the bank's building, who was also a customer of mine, entered the lunchroom. Clearly distraught, his mutterings were not initially understandable, but as he repeated his words and pointed upward, I began to understand.

He was telling me that he needed help. He had just found Diane, his secretary/bookkeeper, lying under her desk in his office. And she wasn't moving! And she had a plastic bag over her head! He was so shocked at the discovery that he hadn't touched her and did not know whether she was alive. And he was so unnerved, he couldn't go back to check on her.

I told him to call 911, and I ran up the stairs to his office.

I found Diane still lying under her desk, fully clothed, with her head furthest under, making it difficult to check her breathing. But I could see the tightly tied string, securing the plastic bag around her neck, eliminated her ability to breathe. Upon checking her cold, clammy wrist, I found no pulse.

The rescue squad arrived shortly and attempted resuscitation — to no avail. The body was removed, and my customer was interviewed by the police. "Apparent suicide" was the initial determination, which was confirmed days later. No note was found.

Why did she choose suicide? She was young, with plenty of life yet to live. An investigation determined that she had "borrowed" an unauthorized $10,000 from Sam and had apparently chosen the certainty of death rather than the shame and uncertainty of facing Sam and the authorities.

Senseless!

It kind of ruins the day!

Jan 1993 Mom Passes I was again enjoying Campbell's soup (chicken noodle and sodium) from the bank's vending machine when Carol called. As she tried to tell me what had happened, her crying immediately told me

Mom had passed suddenly.

She had risen at her usual time, enjoyed her usual breakfast, and then told Carol she wasn't feeling well, laid on her bed, and quietly expired.

Like other war widows, she had struggled with depression since the death of her husband. At times, she felt good, but most times she felt defeated — just hanging on for whatever was to come next. In her depression, she had refused the US Government's offer to return our father's remains for burial at home, leaving him interred in an American military cemetery in the Philippines.

We kids don't understand the decisions a depressed parent makes, but we are affected by those decisions. Mom had made many decisions over the years. Some turned out good. Some turned out otherwise. But one constant was that she always placed her children's best interests first.

Mom deserved the comfort which finally came during the last few years of her life, and she died, likely of an (unconfirmed) sudden stroke.

January 8, 1993, at age 77, Mom had gone with God after a long and challenging journey. Her's was a job well done!

Feb 1993 Discovered in Mom's Belongings In the days following mom's passing, Carol and I endured the task of organizing her personal effects and papers. What we found was rewarding, especially the military records and letters from colleagues and friends of our father.

The following letter and citation package was accompanied by the Silver Star and the Purple Heart medals…

****

10 October 1945

The President of the United States takes pride in presenting the SILVER STAR MEDAL posthumously to

ENSIGN HARRY PATRICK, UNITED STATES NAVAL RSERVE

for service as set forth in the following

CITATION:

" For conspicuous gallantry and intrepidity as Officer-in-charge of the LCT (6) 729, operating against enemy Japanese forces off Corregidor in the Philippine Islands, February 16, 1945. Undeterred by withering enemy machine-gun and rifle fire during initial assault operations, Ensign Patrick skillfully maneuvered his craft through heavy underwater obstructions, to make a successful landing which insured the delivery of vital supplies to our forces. Mortally wounded by a Japanese shell when his vessel struck the beach, Ensign Patrick, by his determined, tireless efforts and daring courage throughout the hazardous operations, had contributed immeasurably to the success of an important mission and his unwavering devotion to duty throughout was in keeping with the highest traditions of the United States Naval Service. He gallantly gave his life for his country."

For the President,

James Forrestal
Secretary of the Navy

****

These are examples of the many letters we found in her files...

Thursday March 1, 1945

Dear Mrs. Patrick,

...how sorry we are about your husband... he was my commanding officer... you have every reason to be proud for his service to our country as a naval officer... he was a wise and intelligent commanding officer who had a really "navy" ship without making his men feel bullied or overburdened with work... this is something only a real leader can do... his character, good humor, and pleasant disposition made all those under his command devoted to him...Though he fully realized the danger involved, he directed his ship through heavy machine gun fire without hesitation or question... he landed his ship at the proper place and delivered a cargo that the Army was in critical need of... just after landing was made, a machine gun bullet struck your husband... *(remainder of letter is missing)*

****

March 12, 1945

My dear Mrs. Patrick,

I was seriously grieved when I learned that your husband had been killed... we had very much in common. I also have two children, am about his age and we had plenty to talk about. It was only the night before the landing that he had invited some of us fellows over to his ship and we had a most pleasant evening - talking mostly of home and the ones we love... we still speak of it as "Patrick's ship"... He was a brave fellow and took that ship right up to the shores of Corregidor without fear of personal danger. It took a brave man to do that... Your husband did not suffer very long. Harry died gallantly... It seems unfair that a man with a family should be deprived of the happiness that would have been his upon his return home... I could tell from our conversations that he loved his family... I feel deprived of what was becoming a steadfast friendship. His loss is a loss to our group, and all the officers and men who knew him (and he had ever so many friends) share your sorrow.

Sincerely yours,

A. A. Andreae
LT (j.g.) USNR

****

The Upjohn Company

April 14, 1945

Dear Mrs. Patrick:

...Harry was my friend and fellow worker. I was very fond of him. We had many good times together and we all looked forward to seeing him at our meetings...it is very hard for me to say anything to you that would be of encouragement or relieve an aching heart. May God bless you and your babies and give you strength to carry on.

Very sincerely yours,

W. P. Ford
Omaha, Nebraska

****

We were also surprised at the extensive personal writings we found in mom's diary...

"How could my world collapse on such a beautiful day?

The children were playing outside, and I was finishing the day's housework and listening to Martha Bohlson's daily tips on how to make a house a better home. I had talked to my parents earlier in the day on the telephone and heard the latest news about our friends and relatives around the family farm. In spite of the problems plaguing the country, everyone was doing well and families were happy together. Our farmer relatives were making plans for spring planting and were again looking forward to seeing all the relatives at the annual family reunion, where everyone wants to see how children grew, meet new family members, learn of upcoming weddings, and listen to my father, "Pop" Weaver, curse both the Democrats and the Republicans. Uncle Ben would know just what to say to get Weaver even madder about the politicians, and the madder he got, the more he would curse. Soon the mothers would be shooing their children away from the men, so the children wouldn't learn any new words.

I greatly enjoy the family reunions which allow me to show off my children. They are so smart and handsome. Carol looks much like her father, and I marvel at the resemblance. Both father and daughter have soft, dark, beautiful, brown hair and blue-gray eyes, like the rest of the Patrick family. I often wonder what the years ahead will hold for my daughter. I worry she might inherit Harry's husky physique — good for a man but not attractive for a woman. But I know I can help her deal with these types of problems and prepare her to overcome any obstacles life presents. I am looking forward to the growth years ahead for Carol.

Michael is a different child. He more resembles my side of the family, with big brown eyes and dark brown hair. He is always into mischief. I remember the night he tested his father. They had been playing in the living room and having the greatest of times. Harry loved to play with the children and would always make a special effort to spend time with them before he did his evening paperwork. This particular night, playtime had passed, and Harry was busy working at his desk. A special picture of Harry sat on the desk. It was a picture he had sent home to me. Michael wasn't ready to quit playing when Harry was, so he threw a marble to get Harry's attention. It broke the glass on the picture and provoked Harry into giving discipline in the form of a spanking. While Michael never threw another marble, the spanking became the only memory he had of his dad.

I lay on the bed and remembered when we had moved into the house. It was such a little house, with only two bedrooms and the smallest of kitchens. But it sat on a large lot, with many fruit trees in the yard and a farmer's field behind the orchard. The field reminded me so much of the farm where I grew up, and I loved our house dearly. Harry had wanted the fruit trees especially because they also reminded him of the house where he grew up. We were very happy in our little house.

I remember when we visited the farm to tell my parents about the house we were buying. We wanted to share our excitement with them. That was a great day! Many of our relatives were there, also, and we took many pictures with Harry's new camera. He wore his Navy uniform, and the kids and I wore our Sunday-best outfits. Sparky, our dog, was also newly washed and brushed for the occasion.

That was a very special day for many reasons — the house, the pictures, and the going-away party. Harry didn't have to join the service, but he felt it was the right thing to do. He enlisted and, with his pharmacy degree, I believed he would serve as a Navy pharmacist and never see combat. The Navy offered him that job, but he declined. The Navy's newest Ensign wanted to serve where he felt he would be doing the most good for his country. He chose combat duty and was trained as an LCT commander. He told me this was what he wanted to do, and I should not worry. He knew I would worry, but he wanted me to not know the real hazards of his assignment.

I tried not to worry that day. It was a busy day, with the work, the pictures, and the party. Everyone seemed happy. My brother, Dillon, and his wife, Grace, were also there. Dillon had enlisted in the Army but didn't yet know what his assignment would be. Dillon loved my children and was always doing special things for them. Everyone had a great day!

I think Harry bought the house so I would feel more secure while he was away, although he didn't say so. Friends offered advice on how I would keep busy with the children and the house and that the war would be over and time would pass so quickly that Harry would be home almost before I realized he was gone. We laughed at how fast the war would be over after Harry and Dillon got involved. I told him I would save some housework for him to do, since he would be back so soon.

After the well-wishing was done, we had started home. Harry was a hunter, like most kids growing up in a rural area. He would always look for game whenever we were in the country, and that night was no exception. Although we were in a hurry to get home, Harry watched closely for rabbits as we sped along the gravel road. Carol had fallen asleep in the back seat, and Michael was perched up high behind me so he could help his father look for rabbits. Suddenly, Harry saw a rabbit and stomped on the brake pedal as he was grabbing his shotgun. In one terrible instant, I heard Michael shrieking. When the car stopped so suddenly, he had plummeted forward like a shot and hit the window post with his nose. Blood gushed everywhere, but Harry didn't even realize what had happened. Damned rabbits!

On that day, I only thought of how stupid and foolish Harry had been for having caused the accident. That evening, one of the last I had with Harry, was not pleasant. Although I knew it hurt Harry just as much as it hurt me to hear Michael cry, I somehow couldn't forgive him for causing his son's pain.

Many memories passed quickly through my mind as I lay on the bed. I wondered if Harry had ever forgiven me for not forgiving him for Michael's' pain. Now, I would never be able to tell Harry I had forgiven him. Again, I cried violently, and someone came into the bedroom to comfort me. I don't even know who it was. The pain was so deep, I still didn't recognize what was happening around me. When I wasn't crying, I was remembering — and both the crying and the remembering were painful. I felt I couldn't go on living.

I remember the day we purchased our furniture. Harry had not yet enlisted, so we felt we could afford good quality furniture. We agreed it would have to last a very long time, and we laughed when we agreed to keep it even through our retirement. When we realized the furniture we wanted still couldn't be afforded on Harry's salary, we were ready to settle for something less. But we were still committed to keeping it through our retirement.

My father had made sure his children learned the value of a hard day's work and how anything worth doing was worth doing well. Much of the furniture in my father's house was hand-made by his father, and it was made to last forever. Even Neva, my father's third wife (he was widowed twice), could not persuade him to buy any new pieces. Harry's father had similar values, so we knew our new furniture would also have to last forever.

Although it took our parent's help financially, we eventually got the furniture we really wanted.

As I looked at the bedroom furniture, I didn't think about how long it would last — but only about the fun we had buying it. We did it together, but now I had no husband with whom to share it.

I cried…"

****

Feb 1993 More From Mom's Diary…..

"It has been nearly a month since the doorbell rang and all the relatives and neighbors came. I still hurt, and still the tears come often. The children seem to be getting along ok, although I don't see them often, as they are staying on the farm with their great aunt and uncle. Everyone thought it would be better for me to be alone and to rest for a while, so several relatives offered to care for the children temporarily. The children chose the farm, for they love it as much as I do. I was sure they would be more comfortable there, because I was afraid I couldn't give them the love and care they needed right then. I wasn't able to think of anything or anyone but Harry.

A boxed flag and three, ugly boxes were delivered since then and sit untouched in the basement. I don't want them opened yet. I know, without looking, what they contain, and I don't want the pain and hurt that will come from seeing the contents. I can wait.

I am in no hurry…"

From her diary, I learned more about the mother I knew and the man/father I had never known, and the short life they shared together.

Mar 1993 The Terrifying Telephone What you never want to hear during a sound sleep — the telephone rang at 3:15 AM.

Favorite daughter explained she had been involved in the accident of a van rolling over on the interstate, in Western Nebraska, while returning to Chicago with a college group on a ski and balloon trip in Colorado.

Fortunately, she was uninjured, and there were no fatalities, but there had been injuries to others in the three-van caravan.

She and two friends were continuing their trip on a train, with a stopover in Big Town at 6:00 AM.

We met them with hugs and food for their continuing journey to Chicago.

Question: Why hadn't she previously informed her parents that she was going on a ski trip?

Hmmm?

1993 Another Day Ruined On a beautiful spring day weeks later, I was diligently working in my office when Tony P entered and asked if I knew where our Director of Human Resources, Norma, might be. His concern was that it was day two of her absence from the office, and she had not notified him such would be the case. Tony had tried to reach her by telephone — to no avail. I knew nothing of her whereabouts, so after discussing possibilities, we decided to visit her house to see if she was ill.

Norma lived in a very nice condo, located on the lake's shore. When she didn't answer our knock on the door, the condo maintenance man opened her door and accompanied us on a search of her home. Everything was in order, as we would have expected of Norma.

We then rushed to her garage, our anxiety increasing.

We did not wait for a locksmith to arrive. We directed the maintenance man to break the lock. As the garage door lifted, the chrome, rear bumper of her recently purchased, always spotless Cadillac, ownership to which she had long aspired, appeared first, then the trunk, and, finally, the rear window, through which we could see a person in the driver's seat. I moved forward and opened the car door. There was Norma, fully clothed, a smile on her face, clutching a picture to her bosom of her and her boyfriend, warmly embraced. Checking for a pulse on her very cold, clammy wrist, I found none.

Appropriate authorities were notified. They later reported the Cadillac's gas tank was empty. No note was found. "Apparent Suicide" was the final confirmed cause of death.

Why did she choose suicide? We could only guess she was despondent over the recent death of her long-time boyfriend. With Norma's approaching retirement date, they had planned on touring the country in his Winnebago, enjoying the remainder of their lives together. Suddenly, he was gone. Norma had no other family. She apparently felt no reason for living.

Why suicide? Fear? Depression? Medical reasons? Makes no sense to me!

I hope to never again need to check for a pulse on somebody's cold and clammy wrist!

Nov 1997 Congratulations! Our still favorite daughter graduated from college, with an employment future somewhat assured, as a Physical Therapist (every family needs a medical professional for the guidance and free advice).

1998 Feeling Great Again! I experienced that elusive "Good Feed!" feeling again at a bank's officer vs staff softball game when batting last in the bottom of the ninth. With 2 outs and the score tied, I drove in the winning run with a single into center field — a walk-off! I can still hear the team cheering —

Good hit! Good hit! Good hit!

Every life deserves at least a couple such thrills!

Remember this lesson when someone close to you needs a little praise. It will make a great difference in both your lives.

1998 Not Again! Working with Tony P, job satisfaction was good. But after all those years of successfully turning a "bad" bank into a "very good" bank came a surprise announcement — the bank had been sold!

The acquiring bank was soon acquired by an even larger bank. Executive management would now come from the distant offices of the larger bank, and, in 1999, Tony, I, and other executives were no longer needed.

After a year in an interim position, I was given the choice of twelve months' severance pay or a comparable job in Portland, Oregon. I gladly accepted the twelve months pay and departed.

DW was not pleased with the news!

1999 Bad Decision I soon found **Job #22** as President of a small community bank located nearby. This bank was owned by yet another, multi-state holding company, and after two years, my "informed, insightful" disagreements with the CEO's directives on many issues led to my termination.

Pitiful four weeks' severance pay!

DW was not pleased with the news!

Justice was served within a year when the FDIC forced the sale of the holding company and its banks due, I suspect, to management malfeasance at the home office.

2000 Pro Golfers Best friend and best man at our wedding, Dave, after 30 years US Army service, had retired at rank of Colonel and moved back to his hometown with Phyllis, his second wife. Because we live 250 miles apart, we usually meet only 3-4 times a year — usually for golf and/or college reunions. He insists on keeping score in order to maintain his handicap record (and to embarrass me).

Dave keeps a bottle of aged Irish whiskey to be opened and consumed at the grave of whoever passes first — he or me.

2001 Next Position I was hired as a First Vice President to start a commercial lending program at a large regional bank nearby.

Despite a daily 120 mile round trip, **Job #23** was a good situation.

DW was pleased with the news!

9/11/2001 AMERICA ATTACKED!! Like most veterans, I polished my combat boots and prepared for the worst!!

Like most older veterans, I wasn't called!

Like most Americans, I prayed for those who were called!

2002 Wedding Bells Our still favorite daughter married Chuck 11/23/2002.

Chuck is a CPA. I finally had someone in the family to visit with about debits and credits.

Hooray!! So exciting!!

DW was pleased!

Aug 2005 Lights and Sirens! A highlight of my employment at this regional bank was the annual bank golf event, where I suffered a heart event, netting a 120 mile ride back to Big Town in an ambulance, lights and siren, and the insertion of four stents.

Apparently, the dietary changes DW forced upon me years earlier were not as effective as was hoped. Or, perhaps the blockages were the result of the tasty food choices I made when DW wasn't looking!

Regardless, I beat the widow-maker just in time and returned to work soon thereafter.

DW was pleased!

2009 God Speed! Marian W passed. Denis W's everlasting grieving began.

2010 Incompetence and Greed After my nine-year employment anniversary, the regional bank suffered the same fate as had been suffered by my previous employer and was closed by the FDIC on June 4, 2010.

As happened at my previous employer, this bank's management had also declined my many informed, insightful suggestions!

Having become the largest bank failure in our state's history, no severance was available.

At age 69, an age with few opportunities for jobless bank executives, my next career position became retirement at home

DW saw mixed blessings with this news!

Then my last, and best, **Job, #24**, began as an on-call nanny for three wonderful grandchildren.

2010 Career Summary I have worked since I was 7 years old; I entered a banking industry that was undergoing tremendous change and disruption nationally; I enjoyed, and/or learned from, every job.

My new job as part-time nanny is the best! While both really enjoying and learning, I hope to impart some useful life lessons to the grands.

2010 Doing My Part   After 41 years of DW handling virtually all the needed housekeeping, shopping, and parenting, we discovered that, with time and opportunity, I could adequately perform some of those same tasks. After all, "I live here, too!"

So, a next new phase of life began.

"As you wish!" became my mantra.

DW was greatly pleased!

(ORP man was domestically challenged)

2011 And then it began!   Cancer!! — followed by radiation treatments!

Signs of aging? No! I'm still a youthful, energetic 70!

Sep 2012 First Love - Gone   The news was difficult to hear!

At what was the beginning of a highly anticipated, though delayed, 50-year, grade school reunion, which should have been only an enjoyable evening of sharing memories of the All Saints graduating class of 1955, my classmate and lifelong friend, Don S, informed me my high school-into-college sweetheart, Sally, had, just the prior week, entered hospice.

Contributing to Sally's declining health was COPD. She didn't smoke until we met, and she never quit.

Cause and effect, I wonder?

Although Sally's path and mine through life had taken different directions since we parted, the memories of our first love remained.

A tearful, long distance telephone call provided our final communication.

Sally passed 9/11/12 after having lived a fruitful, God-centered 71 years. I grieved.

2013 Need 4 Speed   I've seen this in my grandchildren. Each grandchild (boy, girl, boy) has crashed when prematurely going to warp speed in the early stages of learning to ride a bicycle. "Speed" must be in our genes.

Most of my high speed experiences, other than those sanctioned motorcycle races, have come on public streets — roller skates, scooters, bicycles, motorcycles, and automobiles. Some have been near death experiences (really), and I continued to foolishly stretch the rules of common-sense driving in spite of recognizing how only God's hand and Henry have enabled me to narrowly escape so many disasters.

At age 72, I enjoyed the "Rusty Wallace Experience" at the Iowa Speedway near Newton, Iowa. Man, that was fun! Eight laps around a 7/8 mile, concrete, banked track at unregistered but "feels like" g-force speeds in a "retired" NASCAR sprint car!

For only $140, in the provided crash helmet and fire suit, I was buckled in and sped off (after embarrassingly killing the engine twice) for an education in racing. I learned sprint cars have no power-assisted steering or brakes, and the small diameter steering wheel increases the level of driving difficulty. When I first needed the brakes to avoid rear-ending a slower car, I learned how hard it is to stop a sprint car without power brakes! Not like stopping a power-assisted Cadillac!

It seemed patently reckless of the sponsoring company to allow drivers of varying skill levels to play on a racetrack simultaneously with others of similarly deficient, driving skill levels.

In preparation, the "racers" were required to attend a 45-minute classroom "drivers' meeting," where the emphasis was placed on how to keep the ear buds in our ears, because, once on the track, the only supervision comes from a spotter's voice received via the ear buds. Dangerously, of course, the ear buds slip off the ear while driving due to the poorly fitted crash helmets, leaving the spotter's instructions virtually un-hearable.

(I did vaguely hear "Get off the "*%&#*^ track!" from my enraged spotter when I stopped on the track after missing the pit row exit lane.)

My #21 car stayed glued to the concrete in all corners, and I increased speed each lap. The challenge was to not go so fast that the rear end of the car would break loose and come around. The walls of the speedway were punctuated with scars from those drivers who had previously lost control, crashed their cars, and had to pay for the repairs. Although I sensed I was a superstar at warp speed, I likely had not exceeded an embarrassingly slow 80 mph.

Some of the experience was memorialized on film by my race fans — nephew Kelly, his wife Janise, and best friend Dave R. Pics were posted on Facebook.

Then, I took my "need" back to the street.

Grandkids! Pay attention! **Life Lesson**...

Do as I say, not as I do!

Control the "need" — go 4 slow!

Nov 2013 Life's End In a modest room, in a noiseless facility, life ended. I wasn't there. I only heard later that a final, deep breath was sounded, and then she lay still.

A life of medical challenges preceded that final moment. She fought every one of them, but each one left her a little weaker and with another list of pills intended to extend her life and provide some sort of relief from suffering. The quad by-pass, the pacemakers, the diabetes, the cancer, the kidney disease, the peripheral neuropathy — each malady added yet another hill to climb.

Each new hill was met with a goal to be achieved. In the final months, her only goal was to live long enough to meet her new great granddaughter and to attend her son and daughter-in-law's marriage re-commitment ceremony. Sadly, these goals were not met.

I was with her during her final hospital stay when the hospitalist MD brusquely made it clear to her that she was very near death — that her organs would slowly shut down — and there was nothing medical science could do for her until then except attempt to make her comfortable. A tear had rolled down her cheek, but she had expected the news and was ready to accept it. Her fight for life was nearly over. Her concerns now were to make final provisions for her family and her soul. A hastily called meeting with her attorney provided for her family. A hastily called meeting with her priest prepared her soul.

A transport team provided an unintentionally painful and final ride in an ambulance — this time to a hospice facility. The hospice nuns, with well-practiced and oft-repeated efficiency, made her as comfortable as possible, sympathetically ignoring her cries of pain in the process. Initial injections of pain killers were completed, with offers to provide as many pain relieving injections as needed for her to pass comfortably. Although the nuns were sincerely well-intentioned, we observers did not believe the injections came soon, or often, enough.

Then, it was just a matter of time.

During that time, she was unable or unwilling to speak. All of her sounds were groans and cries of pain. I will forever remember her facial expressions during that time — like she was pleading for my help and couldn't understand why I didn't help. But the best I could do was hold her hand, kiss her cheek, and ask the nuns for another injection.

Time of death cannot be precisely predicted. I had returned to my home, taking a few moments to refresh, before returning to the facility, and her son and daughter-in-law had briefly left her side to run a needed errand. She probably did not realize we weren't there, but we will always carry guilt for being absent. The two neighborhood ladies who were present when she passed provided the description of her final moment.

Carol died November 19, 2013, at age 73, without family at her side.

The church funeral was small — just a few relatives from all sides of the family and a few special friends. Throughout her battle, Carol had always made a weekly visit to her beautician, or the beautician would visit her at home or in the hospital. The beautician now prepared Carol's hair for the funeral ceremony. Carol's daughter-in-law coordinated the service and burial clothing. All attendees said how good Carol looked in the casket.

Although the officiating Catholic priest initially resisted Carol's wish to have Willie Nelson's recorded version of "Amazing Grace" played during the ceremony, he relented when told how important it was to her. Carol's best friend for life, Kay, provided the eulogy. Several non-Catholics, contrary to the priest's instructions, received Holy Communion along with the Catholics. Carol would have been proud of them all!

The entombment went well. The officiating priest repeated his meaningful (but forgettable) homily. A typically nice lunch (breaded fried chicken with cake for dessert) back at the church was provided by the ladies guild. Everyone attending renewed acquaintances.
Then, it was over…

Mom and Carol now reside in adjoining crypts — their earthly journeys completed.

Nov 2013 Eulogy Not Given I had prepared this eulogy for Carol but deferred to her best friend, Kay, who gave a most outstanding eulogy, a transcript of which, however, is not available, and which, like many commencement speeches, would soon be forgotten by most attendees.

Thus, I now present my "eulogy not given" —

On behalf of Carol's family, I thank you for being here with us in this difficult time. I know Carol would appreciate you now as she did during her lifetime.

At the risk of omitting someone special, we especially thank a few friends who helped make Carol's last several months bearable — Kay, a lifetime friend, who spent many hours visiting Carol and running errands for her; Janise's mother, Phyllis, who provided extraordinary in-home care for Carol in recent weeks; Pat and Mary, next door neighbors who went far beyond neighborly duty to assist Carol many times; Clara Ann, who kept a watchful eye for any of Carol's needs, delivered the mail and paper daily, and kept Carol's many plants and flowers watered and alive; Marlas, a golfing buddy, who kept watch on Carol and with whom Carol shared many past adventures; Bev and Norma, who made Carol's beauty shop experience a highlight of each week and who brought that experience to Carol's house or to her hospital room when she could not get to their shop; Cousin Jerel, who was always available to help during Carol's many hospital stays; and the many others who helped Carol through the days, weeks, and years of difficult health.

In recent weeks, Carol and I, brother and sister, reminisced mostly about our youth together. We remembered the battles — contesting who would get the 2nd bedroom in our small 2 bedroom house vs. who would sleep on the living room couch; whether the radio would be tuned to that awful country music or to that sweet, cool jazz; who would get to smoke the longest and freshest cigarette butts recovered from the ash tray when Mom wasn't watching; or who would represent the family at the weekly block rosary vs. who would get to stay home with Mom and watch Uncle Miltie.

And we remembered the trouble we got into when we painted the kitchen furniture a bright Chinese red while Mom was at work; and we remembered how our mother taught us a lesson about our responsibility to wash the breakfast dishes — by serving our evening meal on that day's unwashed breakfast dishes; and we remembered some of the many, many other conflicts that naturally arise between brother and sister.

Without going into great detail, suffice it to say Carol suffered health problems throughout her life. In spite of those problems, she endured and moved forward.

Carol provided loving care for our mother in Mom's later years. She enjoyed the many experiences of being the mother of a son whose marriage produced two beautiful granddaughters, a "perfect" great granddaughter, and will soon produce another great grandchild.

Carol loved her family and cared for them as any great mother would.

In recent weeks, as Carol continued her battle to live long enough to welcome the next great grandchild into this world, God had a different plan. Carol finally relented and made her own difficult, but brave, decision to move to hospice after the doctors told her there was nothing else they could do for her. The pain had finally become too great for her to continue fighting.

In most respects, hospice is difficult for both patient and family, in that its mission does not include curing the patient. Yet, when there is nothing that can be done curatively, its mission of providing comfort is welcomed.

We will all miss Carol, yet her passing is in accordance with God's plan, and we must believe that she has earned, and has now received, her heavenly reward.

I miss you, Carol. You were a great sister!

Nov 2013 Epilogue After a funeral, the deceased usually leaves some work to be done by the surviving family members. In Carol's case, some accumulation of material goods occurred during her 73 years. Liquidating her physical assets and managing the funds in her estate required some time and effort, but it was accomplished without additional trauma to any of those family members.

This epilogue is my personal reflection on the state of hospice as I experienced it with Carol.

For a person needing frequent blood transfusions to extend life, there comes a point where politics, informed by medical science, dictates such treatments are for naught and entering hospice becomes appropriate. All curative treatments then become unavailable under strict hospice rules, including that if the "victim" of such rules, hoping to live even a few more days, receives a transfusion after entering hospice, the "victim" is removed from hospice, and all hospice financial benefits are then terminated. Such happened to Carol in her desire to live a few more days/weeks in order to meet her soon-to-be-born great granddaughter. Unaware of this hospice rule, she did receive such a transfusion, which extended her life a few more hours but, sadly, not long enough to meet her new great granddaughter. This action threw her family into another bureaucratic quagmire, making the time of her dying even more stressful.

I can't comprehend why a life sustaining procedure, such as a transfusion (if the blood is available and not needed elsewhere), is prohibited in favor of watching life slowly drain from the body.

On a related matter, regarding the companies which provide home hospice care, Carol's family's experience, unfortunately, saw only high cost and poor service from a grossly unqualified staff!

Fortunately, most patients need these services for only a very short time.

2013 Reflecting on Her Last Years As I had counseled her on investments, her only major concern was that she should never be poor again. Thus, for 25 years, the trust funds were, mostly, very conservatively invested in a ladder of US Government securities and FDIC-insured certificates of deposit. A more aggressive investment of a small portion of those funds was then invested in common stocks and traded frequently, and the trust fund balance continued to increase, substantially exceeding the amount Carol originally received from the lawsuit.

But for Carol's pain, suffering, and money, all resulting from the injury, many things would be different today. Her conservative $3500 monthly withdrawal from the trust was more than sufficient for living and paying routine expenses (and she never requested more). And, of course, the state and federal taxing authorities enjoyed the significantly increased personal taxes she then had to pay on the trust's earnings.

The money helped other family members, as well. Carol funded a down payment large enough to allow her son and daughter-in-law to purchase a new home. She helped pay for my favorite daughter's over-priced undergraduate and graduate degrees. She funded college educations for her two granddaughters. And, of course, she gave numerous, smaller financial gifts to non-profits and other individuals along the way to help support and sustain lifestyles they could never have otherwise afforded.

Just think of how things might have been without Carol's fateful and painful injury. Her son & daughter-in-law might still be living in the very cramped trailer house; my daughter might not have attained her high-quality education and the resulting advantages that have accrued; Carol and Mom might never have escaped sub-standard housing; I would have been economically stretched to provide some financial support to Carol and Mom, negatively impacting my ability to adequately support my own family.

Many things would have, undoubtedly, been different without Carol's painful injury and successful lawsuit. Sadly, the funds did nothing to alleviate her lifelong back pain.

Or, who knows, things could have turned out better. Only God knows.

(Note — Subsequent to her death, the trust continues to provide loving financial support to Carol's beneficiaries.)

2013 God Speed! Margaret P passed. Tony P feels lost.

2013 Ronnie — A Longtime Friend After having learned belatedly of my sister's death, Ronnie T contacted me via face-time from his home in Reno and invited me to visit there.

Over many years, he had suffered debilitating injuries from motorcycle accidents and, as a result, infrequently traveled.

Many years had passed since we had been together. After remotely sharing many memories, I committed to visiting him sometime in the future.

2014 God Speed! Friend and mentor, Gene B, passed.

Gene B always created a fun working environment for his staff. During the cool weather days, he kept a readily available bottle of liqueur on the outside window ledge of our department. Reasons to celebrate any occasion or success were often and easy.

Early in our acquaintance, I thought Gene perhaps celebrated too often, as walking next to him was always hazardous. He would walk in a wobbly manner, which I later learned was because he had a glass eye, having lost his biological eye in a childhood accident. After learning this, I declined his many offers to fly with him in his single-engine Cessna. Those who accepted his invitation always reported an experience they preferred to not repeat.

Some years later, Gene stopped piloting when, accompanied by his wife and two children, a disaster was narrowly avoided during a difficult landing.

During the years of our "second tour" together, unlike the culture at The Central Bank, holiday parties were not supported by this bank's management. Historically, years before, the parties had gotten too crazy and had become a liability to their careers, so management replaced bank-sponsored, "traditional" holiday parties with cookies and apple cider refreshments, served in the employee lunchroom during office hours. While these holiday refreshments were certainly "nice", having enjoyed the more "traditional" holiday parties in prior years at The Central Bank, Gene and I decided to provide our small Controllers Department staff a more "traditional," evening holiday party, at our own expense (paid 2/3 he and 1/3 me).

Our parties were more in the "tradition" of the "have fun, don't tell" parties of old. One notable year, at an upscale restaurant, found Gene, after dinner and many drinks, crawling around on hands and knees under the dinner table, kissing the ankles of our female staff. I do not recall how that evening ended — nor would I tell if I did!

Fast forward to 1975, when sizable losses in the bank's loan portfolio caused new management to take over the bank, resulting in a loss of local career opportunities for Gene and other senior managers. He accepted a transfer to a new position in Big City. Likely feeling career-stunted, and with business and personal marital challenges, Gene left the new position after a few months and took a career opportunity in Texas. I did not follow.

Gene had met and married his second wife, Faye, while in Big City. Their personal and business careers flourished while in Dallas, and then they retired to Austin, where Gene could play golf every day — on his own time and dime. Years later, they continued their retirements in Seattle.

We reunited briefly when they passed through Big Town in 2002 and were special guests for a social evening at Tony and Margaret P's home. Along with several former associates, including Gene E and Norm L, memories were shared and laughs enjoyed. Such was the last time I saw Gene, and he seemed to be in great health and spirits. A few annual telephone visits with Gene occurred after that (he always asked especially about DW and our favorite daughter) with the last visit being in early 2014. He never mentioned having health problems.

Surprised when I opened it, the email came from Faye, disclosing Gene had been painfully ill the past year with an auto-immune disease, Wegener's Granulomatosis, and had passed 11/20/14. I immediately replied with a short email, expressing my shock and sadness at his passing, and asked for more details and about arrangements. Because I received no more information from Faye, I searched for an obituary in Seattle's on-line local papers — but found none.

My friend and mentor was gone, and I had had no opportunity to again express my appreciation for his years of personal guidance.

Further efforts to contact Faye were unsuccessful.

St. Peter surely received a seasoned and competent Controller.

Jun 7, 2014 Hot Pop! DW and I celebrated 45 years of marriage. It had been 49 years since I had owned one, so I felt deserving. I purchased a new Honda motorcycle today. Grandkids think I'm "cool."

DW was not pleased.

(ORP man was perplexed)

2015 Last Visit with a Longtime Friend I never got to see Ronnie in Reno. However, I did visit him and his father, Don T, in Hometown. Ronnie had returned home to visit his 93-year-old father, who had recently suffered a fall and was residing in a nursing home. While there, Ronnie suffered a stroke and was placed in a different nursing home, miles from his father.

Mutual friends Gregory and Dixie R notified me of Ronnie's and Don's situations. Greg and Dixie had taken responsibility for their care, spending many hours assisting with medical and financial issues, selling Don's home, and looking after Ronnie. Greg had also grown up with Ronnie and me, and during his working career Greg's shop had serviced Don's cars. We also enjoyed close connections as motorcycle enthusiasts.

Upon hearing of their situations, I soon visited Ronnie and Don in their respective nursing homes.

Don didn't remember me nor did he seem to realize where he was living. But, according to comments from the female nursing staff, he still featured himself, all 85 pounds, as quite the debonair gentleman. Our visit was brief and, for me, heartbreaking, and I departed hoping my next stop that day, with Ronnie, would be happier.

Greg had previously informed me Ronnie could barely walk and was unable to talk, making only unintelligible sounds of frustration. Knowing that, I took my old racing helmet with me, hoping it would help Ronnie remember me. On the helmet were painted the word "Toad", my nickname commonly used in my late teenage years by my "dark side" friends, and a fair representation of a toad. Ronnie had been instrumental in originally burdening me with that nickname.

When I showed the helmet to Ronnie, he caressed it and cried. I can only hope that his cries evidenced recognition of it and me, and he felt some joy and comfort as a result.

Ronnie enthusiastically showed me his life, via photo album, of people and places he had enjoyed, none of whom I recognized, and after 45 minutes of visiting, filled with many moments of Ronnie's failed verbal efforts and crying, time was up. We embraced with a manly hug, something we would likely have never done in our younger years. I assured him he was going to be ok, and departed — with his tears on my shoulders. I hopefully prayed his health would improve, and we would visit again soon.

Although Ronnie had months previously told me of a health issue (a portion of his foot had been removed due to gangrene), it wasn't until Greg informed me, days after our visit, Ronnie had also been previously diagnosed with Stage 4 prostate cancer and had a failing heart.

Within a few days, Greg and Dixie arranged details and then transported Ronnie back to Reno, where he entered a nursing home, knowing the end was near.

2015 God Speed! Greg called today. My lifelong friend Ronnie passed yesterday. The tears swelled.

2017 Still Hot Pop! DW and I celebrated 48 years of marriage. I traded the Honda for a new Triumph.

DW was not pleased.

Feb 23, 2018 A disappointing day DW and I attended a memorial service for a brother of the aforementioned Kay S. I had never met the brother, so my only reason for attending was to renew my acquaintance with Kay, with whom I had had no contact for 45 years, and to jointly "entertain" DW with Kay's and my shared memories of many, personally important, "The Central Bank" era days and evenings.

To my total disappointment, Kay S neither recognized me nor did she recall the fond memories I placed before her. Her life seemed to have taken a downward spiral.

A highly anticipated reunion produced only hollow emotion. It was as if I had opened a beautifully wrapped box containing my Christmas present — and the box was empty!

2020 Still Sizzling! DW and I celebrated 51 years of marriage in 2020. I traded the Triumph for a new Yamaha.

DW was not pleased.

2021 Bye Bye Hot (Pop) Wheels DW and I celebrated 52 years of marriage. I sold the Yamaha.

All is now at peace in the world.

DW is pleased!

(ORP man is pleased)

2021 Victory! I joyously rang the bell today, signifying my cancer treatments were considered successful and complete!

Jul 10 2021 God Speed! Jon S, my friend, fraternity brother, attorney, and frequent roommate and co-conspirator in many activities, passed after battling overwhelming maladies. His wife, Ann, held his hand at the end.

2021 Prayers Answered! After an eight year battle, my older grandson joyously rang the bell. His cancer is deemed in remission!!!!!!! Best news ever!!!!!!

2022 DW Periodic Retrospective My DW (meaning "Dear Wife," a term borrowed from good friend and former roommate, Jimmy L), has managed all significant parts of my post-bachelor, adult life for the past 53 years. She has guided me through the minefields of life. The results, I believe, are reasonably good and, certainly, much better than I could have done on my own.

When becoming acquainted with new folks socially, the question always arises, "How did you two meet?" Very often, DW responds: "I found him at an antique store!"

Or, she may say we met at a local bar on a Friday evening, after having one-too-many refreshments (oh, those Fridays!).

My version more accurately explains that we met at the bank — but only on a passing basis. No one should misunderstand from her version that she picked me up at the bar — I'm not that kind of guy! But since we did actually engage in our first social conversation at the bar, her version is not without some merit.

"Nonnie" to her three grandchildren, she is an easy touch for them — as it should be.
I could relate many more events and characteristics with/of DW, but I am, no doubt, already in dangerous territory for the foregoing. DW is much more private about her personal life than am I, so I will leave it at this…

God sent me a wonderful person
who has made me a better person in all ways.
I am blest, and I love and thank her! Period!

(Oh! One more thing. Regretfully, I have often lacked thoughtfulness and understanding, and I have never expressed my appreciation sufficiently.)

Aug 15 2022 God Speed! Carma Jean passed. Fred held her at the end. Fred struggles on. DW is devastated.

2022 Embracing Life After several wonderful years on the plains of Colorado, Kelly and Janise, along with their two daughters, three grand daughters, and one grandson, continued their respective journeys and now reside happily in the wooded hills of Tennessee.

Jan 17, 2024 God Speed! After several years of fighting for just one more day, Ron S. succumbed. I couldn't have asked for a better brother-in-law.

Jan 19, 2024 God Speed! At the urging of my wise and thoughtful DW, I visited Jackie in her nursing home suite where she had resided for several years after being brutally beaten by an unknown assailant. Also suffering from COPD, her 77 pound body was nearing its final moments. We enjoyed three visits over two months time, exchanging memories of times gone bye 57+ years ago, and I looked forward to more such visits. Sadly, such was not to be.

DW and I attended her funeral. Though Jackie and I had had no contact all those years, my grief was real.

Jul 4, 2024 God Speed! When Denis W and I visited yesterday, we made plans for attending the next alumni reunion with our third amigo, Dave R. Sadly, it will not happen. Dave and I will carry-on without him.

Nov 12, 2024 God Speed! Lifetime friend, Don S, passed today in the arms of his wife, Joan, surrounded by loving family and friends. Don was a friend at the beginning, the end, and throughout many very important parts of my life. I am very fortunate to have known him.

****

2025 Wasting Time on "What If's"

Peering out through the corner of my eye from under the covers, the digital clock reads 5:39 AM. Unable to blank my mind so I can return to sleep, reflections on my life persist, as they have done so often over the years.

Here I am, in a warm bed, in a nice house, in a nice neighborhood, in a nice town, in a nice state, in a nice country, with a wonderful wife lying next to me — knowing that life has been good, yet being unsettled both by things I have done and things I should have done.

What if my dad had come home instead of those three boxes? How different might our family's lives have been?

Would my Mom and Carol had happier lives?

Would my dad have been proud of me? Did his death become my crutch? Would I have been a better son, brother, husband, friend, person?

Was I a good "man of the house"?

What might my lifetime GPA as a human being be?

These and similar thoughts have visited me periodically throughout my life but have become more frequent as the end of life comes closer, as I realize there are now fewer days, weeks, and years (only God knows how many) in which to shape the final picture of my life.

Does it really matter?

I believe it does matter! Everyone and everything matters. My concerned high school priest/ teacher should have explained it that way.

He should have told me that the results of the choices I would make over my lifetime do matter — and can't be changed.

Yet, my continuous mental examination of my life continues, imagining what I could have done better, as if I can somehow change the results of my past actions.

Do I still have time to repair any deficiencies?

Have I progressed sufficiently toward my goal of eternal salvation?

Has our journey been real or just another dream — a dream that repeats so often, filled with thoughts of family, friends, acquaintances, the past and the future?

All these agonizing "What If's" have changed nothing and are only a waste of time, which should be used only for looking forward.

Only the time on the digital clock has changed.

It is now 5:41 AM, and I am still who and what I am. Perhaps this "man of the house" should just be satisfied with that.

Now, if I can get just one more hour of sleep…

****

Author's Note

Looking Forward

Our fourteen years of retirement have been filled without the pressure of a specific and burdensome schedule, except for the never-ending frequency of doctors appointments caused by a growing list of physical ailments. By physical appearance, we look to be in fairly good health and are quite mobile, only proving physical appearance does not tell the whole story.

Our favorite daughter's family keeps me periodically busy. The three grandchildren, of course, are the best and brightest and are progressing well academically. Daughter and son-in-law appreciate my very non-professional fix-it skills (fix one, break two) manifested at their house. Along with care and maintenance on our own house, there are many opportunities to avoid boredom. Planning for our eventual funerals also takes some time.

Over the years, my original Hometown has faded into the past while original Big Town has become Hometown, and Big City has become Big Big City, where our older grandson now attends college, causing us ongoing concern based on both my past personal experiences there and by the many recurring problems faced by Big Big City residents today. The two other grand kids will likely cause us similar concerns as they grow and leave Hometown. Such is the circle of life.

Voids in my life are strongly felt. Mom, Carol, Sally, Ronnie, Gene, Margaret, Jon, Carma Jean, Ron S, Jackie, Denis W, Don S and others have passed.

DW continues her never-ending, up-hill battle to make me an even better person.

Dave and I continue to meet 3 — 4 times annually for golf.

We don't keep score.

(ORP man rests.)

At a glance -

Once

Upon

a

Time

3 22 '99

TRIGGER

Burgers -
Brats -
Hot Dogs -
Special -
Advil
DOMESTIC
HARD